To Joy —

you may see

new folks

Mike Brown

Enjoy the book,

Jayce!

Patricia A. Floyd

Out *of the* Darkness
Into Light

A Blind Fisherman's Story

E. Michael Lorance

And

Patricia W. Floyd

WestBow
PRESS
A DIVISION OF THOMAS NELSON

Copyright © 2012 E. Michael Lorance and Patricia W. Floyd

All rights reserved. No part of this book may be used or reproduced by any means, graphic, electronic, or mechanical, including photocopying, recording, taping or by any information storage retrieval system without the written permission of the publisher except in the case of brief quotations embodied in critical articles and reviews.

ISBN: 978-1-4497-5853-0 (e)
ISBN: 978-1-4497-5852-3 (sc)
ISBN: 978-1-4497-5851-6 (hc)

Library of Congress Control Number: 2012912224

WestBow Press books may be ordered through booksellers or by contacting:

WestBow Press
A Division of Thomas Nelson
1663 Liberty Drive
Bloomington, IN 47403
www.westbowpress.com
1-(866) 928-1240

Because of the dynamic nature of the Internet, any web addresses or links contained in this book may have changed since publication and may no longer be valid. The views expressed in this work are solely those of the author and do not necessarily reflect the views of the publisher, and the publisher hereby disclaims any responsibility for them.

Any people depicted in stock imagery provided by Thinkstock are models, and such images are being used for illustrative purposes only.

Certain stock imagery © Thinkstock.

Printed in the United States of America

WestBow Press rev. date: 07/11/2012

In memory of Ruby

CONTENTS

CHAPTER 1
The News
1

CHAPTER 2
Early Years
5

CHAPTER 3
Reluctant Hero
11

CHAPTER 4
Troublesome Teens
15

CHAPTER 5
Family
19

CHAPTER 6
Ruby
23

CHAPTER 7
Laddie
27

CHAPTER 8
Fort Lost in the Woods
29

CHAPTER 9
Finding Work
33

CHAPTER 10
The Cabin
39

CHAPTER 11
Seeing Eye
47

CHAPTER 12
Guide Dog Trainers
53

CHAPTER 13
Partners
61

CHAPTER 14
Coping with Blindness
69

CHAPTER 15
Opportunities
79

CHAPTER 16
Television
87

CHAPTER 17
Characters
95

CHAPTER 18
Fishing
107

CHAPTER 19
First Tournament
117

CHAPTER 20
Bass Anglers Sportsman Society
121

CHAPTER 21
Mexico
129

CHAPTER 22
Saint Thomas
133

CHAPTER 23
Heart Attack
137

CHAPTER 24
Living Life Blind
141

PREFACE

The town of Murfreesboro is located between the forks of Stones River—the East Fork and the West Fork—in middle Tennessee. In the 1930s Murfreesboro had a population of about six to eight thousand. Now it is no longer referred to as a town but a city, with a population of around 185,000. It is the home of Middle Tennessee State University, which has the largest undergraduate attendance in the state and has contributed to the rapid growth of Murfreesboro.

Mike Lorance grew up about one mile from the West Fork of Stones River, the site of a major Civil War battle. This book shares his memories of growing up near and around the river and his most favorite pastime—fishing. Mike was the product of a single-parent home due to the divorce of his parents when he was around eleven or twelve years old. He and his sister were pretty much left on their own while his mother was forced to seek work outside the home to support the family.

His childhood was a fairly normal one for a child of the above circumstances other than a couple of heroic deeds due to his close proximity to his beloved water. He received devastating news in his late teens that changed his life in ways we cannot imagine: he was going blind. He is an extraordinary person in that he lives his life as a sighted person and goes about his day-to-day living very much as you or I do. He even fishes and does a better job of it than most fishermen! If he hits a stumbling block, he finds a solution around it without grumbling or complaining about his lot in this world.

Mike lives in the home he and his wife, Ruby, lived in when she was alive. He cooks his own meals, cleans his own house, does his own laundry and all the chores we take for granted. But each of these takes extra effort for him to complete in a satisfactory manner. He is always upbeat, has a wonderful sense of humor, and makes the most of each day given him.

Mike and his sister, Georgia Mai, both went blind in their twenties and had to learn to cope with this handicap. As far as either knows, there is not a history of blindness in their lineage, and neither parent was blind. They were afflicted with retinitis stigmatosis, which is a degeneration of the retina.

Many, many years ago, Mike and I were at a company dinner, and he (as usual) was telling story after story about his exploits. I was very much intrigued with these stories and encouraged him to write a book about his life. Thirty-five to forty years later, my husband, Don, answered the phone, and Mike requested I write the book about his life. Dumbfounded, I said, "Mike, I've never done anything like that in my life!" He said, "I've not either, but let's do it!" That's the type of guy he is.

I have not written this book—Mike has. He continually strives to share his philosophy of life with others and wants to impress upon people to make the most of every situation in order to glean the most out of life. I believe you will embrace that philosophy just a little bit after reading his story. I have a great admiration for him and feel so privileged to have known him.

Patricia W. Floyd

ACKNOWLEDGMENTS

Special thanks to Greg Pogue for his guidance and expertise, which were invaluable in the writing of this book. He helped make sense out of a jumble of stories, found more errors than anyone would care to admit, and gently steered us in the right direction in getting Mike's story told. We have learned so much from him and are grateful for his patience and for always being available. He is an excellent editor, and we consider him a good friend.

Thanks also to Neal Watson, who snapped picture after picture so we would have several from which to choose. His beautiful photographs show his superior artistic talent, as evidenced by the cover.

CHAPTER 1

THE NEWS

I was around twenty-seven or twenty-eight when I began losing my sight. I started running into things, like posts, signs, and even people just walking around in town. People I had known all my life would greet me, and I wouldn't recognize them. I was having a problem holding a job. I ran service stations, I sold furniture, I sold tires, I did everything to try to make a living, but things weren't getting any better.

All the while I was taking these jobs, I noticed that I was having a harder time seeing. Things that I previously could see I could not make out now. It was getting too hard for me to do the job, as my eyes were getting weaker. It was a little harder for me to see in the daytime, but I had no problems at night under the car lights. I went to work at United Cities Gas Company as a salesman and was doing fairly well, but I was having problems, especially in the daytime, when the sun came out. I really couldn't see what I was doing. I was having problems keeping any job. I'd move from one to the other, but since I couldn't see very well, jobs didn't last very long.

Finally, I went to an optometrist in Murfreesboro. He looked at my eyes and asked, "You know what?"

I said, "No, sir."

He replied, "You're going blind." It was a sad day when he told me that. He did not know how long it would be before I would go blind, but he said, "You will probably always be able to get around, because you may have shotgun vision." Shotgun vision is where you have no peripheral vision and can only see toward the center front. I sat there a minute, trying to compose myself, and thought, *Well, what in the world am I going to do?*

Stunned, I left the doctor's office and made my way to where I had parked my car, on the other side of the square. The doctor had dilated my eyes, and I could hardly see anything. There was snow on the ground, the sun was bright, and I was totally blind. I got a little idea of what things might be like in the future.

In all my years, I had never had so much trouble walking about four or five blocks. I ran into buildings, light posts, cars—you name it, I hit it. I had so many bumps and bruises that I looked like I had been beaten. I stumbled and tripped over curbs and cracks in the sidewalk. I'm sure I looked like a person who'd had too much to drink, going this way and that.

I finally reached my car. I sat there quite a long while, trying to absorb what the doctor had revealed to me. I had no idea what I could do or what might happen. I was completely numb, but eventually I began to panic. *How am I going to support my family? How am I going to get around?* Then it really hit me: *How am I going to fish?*

After quite a long time—I really don't know how long—I managed to call my wife at State Farm. She came by a little frustrated because I didn't come and get her. Well, I didn't tell her what was going to happen, even though for several months I had been having quite a hard time. I'd run into things, and people would think I was drunk. When I'd meet people on the street, they'd say, "Ugh," and then they'd tell my wife I'd been drinking. I didn't even drink at all, but everybody thought I did.

The doctor had told me I might have shotgun vision, but that was not the way it was. As I started going downhill, I couldn't see anything in front of me, but I could see to the side.

After about six months, I told my wife. I said, "I haven't told you, but I am going blind. I don't know how quick, but I can't see very well now." She was just as shocked as I was, and her reaction was the same as mine: "What are we going to do?" This was the beginning of some really tough times. It was hard! I had no idea what I was going to do.

CHAPTER 2

EARLY YEARS

I was born in 1932, just outside of Murfreesboro, Tennessee, in the home of Martha and Hershel Lorance and my sister, Georgia Mai. This was a tough time in everyone's life. This was during the Depression, and people didn't have money or very much food, so another mouth to feed was not an exciting occurrence in this family.

The old house we lived in was called the "tollgate house" on Manson Pike. This house had been where the toll was collected as people crossed the bridge over the Stones River. Living across the street from me at that time was Bill Wilson, who later became the sheriff of Rutherford County, and his son, Floyd Wilson, who later became a State Farm agent. We lived in this old tollgate house until I was about three or four years old.

I was approximately four years old, and on Christmas Eve, things at my house were looking really drab. We had very little food and very, very little money. My father had five dollars in his pocket, and he went up to the square in Murfreesboro. He went into this gambling establishment known as the White Front Barber Shop. It was a little illegal, but he went in there anyway. When he came out, he had won a deed to some property over on Battleground Drive, an automobile, and several hundred dollars. In those days, that was a lot of money. Boy, we had a terrific Christmas. My father took that money and built a house on the lot on Battleground Drive. It wasn't a large house, but in those days, we didn't need large houses.

Christmas at my house was never really a festive thing, and in all my years at home, we never had a Christmas tree. One Christmas I wanted a bicycle. Oh, I wanted that little feller so bad. Everybody had bicycles but me. Well, come Christmas morning, I just knew I'd have a bicycle, but my mother said, "Your Christmas present is in the back of the car."

I went out there, and guess what I had? A basketball! I was never so depressed in my life. I said, "Oh man, everybody's got a bicycle, and what have I got? I've got a basketball." Finally, about May or June, my father bought me a bicycle. I was the most excited kid. You'd think Christmas came three or four times a year when I got that bicycle.

When I grew up on Battleground Drive many, many years ago—I guess they named it Battleground Drive because of all the Civil War battles that were fought in this area—we used to walk up and down the road and find minié balls (a type of bullet used in muzzle-loaded guns) everywhere. You could pick them up and shoot them in a slingshot, and now they're worth no telling what. I've probably shot a half a ton of them in a slingshot. There were trenches built all up and down this area. As a matter of fact, not too far from where I lived is where the Battle of Stones River took place.

When I was about ten years old, I had a great attraction to the river. I couldn't swim, but I just had to go to the river. That seemed to be the one thing I really liked to do.

Like I said before, times were hard. My father raised a lot of pigs behind the house. He worked at the Carnation milk plant, and anytime a can went through the machine with a dent in it, the machine would kick it out. So he brought these cans home, and we would feed the pigs Carnation milk and "shorts," which was food for the pigs. We raised probably forty or fifty pigs behind the house for meat and to sell.

I remember one occasion when a pig passed away and left about ten or twelve little piglets. My job was to feed the little pigs. In my anxiety to go fishing one day, I overfed the little pigs, and all but two passed away. It was a very stressful time in my life. I had to go bury nine little pigs, and I treated the two that remained like they were really super pets.

I'm sure everyone has heard, "Well, when I was young, I walked to school." As a matter of fact, I *did* walk to school. We were about a mile and a half from my grammar school, which was Crichlow. We either had to walk to Crichlow or ride to work with my mother and father every morning at five o'clock and stay down in the basement of the courthouse until it was time to go to school. I'm sure bad things would happen if you tried to do that now.

I got out of Crichlow Grammar School and moved over to a building called Cox Memorial. In that building, they had the sixth, seventh, and eighth grades. This is where my life took a turn for the worse. The river continued to call, and whenever I could, I headed for the river.

In those days I could not swim, and there were a lot of guys who would be down there swimming, I said, "Boy, that's easy. I believe I could do that." Guess what? I jumped into the river and couldn't swim a lick. I liked to have drowned until one of my friends pulled me out. That's when I decided that this old boy was going to learn to swim. So I got me a barrel and set it on the sandbar. I could swim underwater but not on top, so I would dive off the barrel and swim underwater over to the bank. I'm glad it wasn't a long distance. Later on, I did learn to swim on top and became quite proficient at it.

Those were also sad times in my life. I was about eleven or twelve years old when my mother and father got a divorce. My mother worked at the Veterans Administration Hospital, and when she would leave to go to work, if I wasn't going to school, I'd hightail it to the river. Being a good mother, when she'd come in the afternoon, she would ask me, "Michael, did you go to the river?"

I could not tell her a story, and I'd say, "Yes, ma'am." So she would whip me.

The next day she'd come in, and I was supposed to mow the yard. But I'd be out there, flying up and down that yard. I'd be cutting that yard like forty dogs, and she'd ask, "Michael, did you go to the river?"

I'd say, "Yes, ma'am." Guess what? She'd spank me again.

My mother didn't know I could swim, and she was afraid I'd go in the river and drown. Since my mother and father's divorce, my mother had to be the provider and this left me without guidance during the day. Anytime anyone drowned or if they'd had any problems on the river, they'd come to my house because everyone always expected me to be involved.

Back in these early times, we'd take a trip to Cedar Forest, now known as Cedars of Lebanon; it is about eighteen miles from Murfreesboro. It was a state park with a big swimming pool. This place was really great, and we didn't get to go that often. We went in there and my mother said, "Don't go in the deep water." But she turned her head, and I dived off into the deep water, and she liked to have had a heart attack. She didn't even know I could swim.

I continued to go to the river every opportunity I'd get. We were in the eighth grade, and Mrs. Sarah Reeves was my teacher. Well, Mrs. Reeves had a little trouble seeing, and when she'd turn her head, I would slip out the back door and go upstairs and play basketball and anything else I could find to do to get me out of class. Then I'd sneak back in the back door, 'cause she couldn't see me.

One day she went out of the room, and I was sitting back there, doing everything I was supposed to do. When she walked back in, there were erasers flying, pencils flying—I wasn't doing anything. She started calling names. She called my friend Floyd Wilson's name. She called my name, and I said, "Mrs. Reeves, I haven't done anything."

She said, "You get in line with everybody else." She took us all up to the office. One by one, we had to lie down across a chair and take a couple of licks. She got to me, and she said, "Lay down across that chair."

I said, "Mrs. Reeves, I haven't done anything."

She said, "You lay down across the chair." I wouldn't do it. She asked, "Where does your father work?"

"I don't know."

"What's his phone number?"

"I don't know."

"Well where does your mother work?"

"I don't know."

"What's her phone number?"

"I don't know."

"Young man, you're going to be expelled for three days."

"Yes ma'am." She sent me home.

Every morning for three days, when my mother would leave to go to work, I'd haul it to the river, but I made sure I got in before she arrived home. My mother didn't find out that I had been expelled from grammar school until I was in my thirties. She then threatened to whip me again.

Another time when I was in my eighth grade, they came around asking for volunteers to help put out shrubbery around Cox Memorial. If you volunteered, you would get to go home for lunch. Well since I lived about a mile from the school, I volunteered.

Every day when I was through, I'd go to Mrs. Reeves and say, "Mrs. Reeves, I'm finished."

She'd say, "Well you go home for lunch." Guess what? I'd go home for lunch, but I couldn't find my way back to school. I would head to the river and go fishing. There would just be a calling, "Go to the river!"

I grew up hard in those days. I didn't have a lot of guidance. My father was gone, and no one was there except my mother, so I pretty well did as I pleased. But anytime there was something to do, it seemed like everybody called on me. I had a next-door neighbor—Ralph Underwood—who did odd jobs for people. He hauled concrete blocks and other things. He would pay me twenty cents to load 250 concrete blocks and twenty cents to unload them. That's how I made my spending money.

Each Saturday there would be a knock on the door, and there would be Mr. Edmond Swain, who lived on Manson Pike. He was looking for somebody to either pull corn or do something to help him on the farm, and I was always elected.

I continued to spend more time on the riverbanks than I did anywhere else. I had this big, old, yellow shepherd dog that went everywhere I went, so I wasn't afraid to run up and down the riverbanks at night. I knew nothing was going to bother me. My mother didn't. She was always on my case about going to the river. I thought I could manage all right, but she didn't think so.

A few years went by, and I became very proficient in fishing. I fished up and down the riverbanks. I waded in the rivers. I knew where every little rock was and hopefully where every little fish was located. I really provided a lot of fish for our family.

Everybody has someone in their family who is a "tattletale." Well in my family, it was my sister, Georgia Mai. Every time I had problems or got into trouble, she'd run home and tell Mother, knowing I was going to get a spanking. One day I got into a little trouble in school, and she'd gone running home to tell Mother. I knew I was going to get a spanking, so I went out, gathered up some books, and put them in my pants. Well I went in, and Mother proceeded to give me a spanking, and I hollered and screamed like you'd think they were killing me.

When she got through, I got up, went outside, and was taking these books out of my pants when my tattletale sister saw me. She asked, "What are you doing?"

I said, "Well, I put these books in my pants, because I didn't want to take a whipping too easy."

So what does tattletale do? She ran in and told my mother. Guess what? I got a return visit—Mother calling, "Michael, come here!" I knew what was going to happen. Well this time it wasn't a put-on. She gave me a really good thrashing.

Before I went blind, I fished just about every area river or stream that you can think of. I waded most of them. When I cross them now, I think, *Well I used to fish right down there, and I know everything that's down there. There are rocks here—there are rocks there and hopefully fish.* You can change what's up and down the river, but it's hard to change the river itself. And if you've ever been there, you pretty well know what's there.

Chapter 3

Reluctant Hero

Fishing was always the foremost thing on my mind. Early one morning in August 1948, I was standing in the far corner of Manson's Dam out on Manson Pike, and across the river, about two hundred feet, was a big rock. I'm sitting there fishing. There's a big bass out there in some rocks above this dam. I'd tackled it a couple of times and had not been successful. He had outwitted me each time, but I knew I had to catch him.

Well I'm there fishing up a storm, and here comes this cab above me. It had this mother and three children in it. They got out, and I watched them as they walked over onto this big rock and started watching me fish. Across the bridge came this truck; this was an old rickety bridge if anybody ever remembers it. I turned to see what was wrong with the bridge and if it was going to fall in, and when I turned back, the mother and the three children were gone.

I started to cast again, assuming they had got up and left, and all of a sudden this head started bobbing up. I thought, *Huh, they're drowning!* So I pulled off my clothes down to my jockey shorts; they were new jockey shorts by the way—my mother had just purchased them. Into the river I went, swimming over there, which was no chore for me at that time. When the jockey shorts got wet, I believe you could fit them over a fifty-gallon drum. Well about halfway out there, they had to go.

So I swam over to the oldest boy, who turned out to be six years old, and put him up on the bank. I turned around and saw the mother, and she had the little girl around her neck. So I swam out there and got her, and pulled her and the little girl up on the bank.

I did not have a stitch on. Nobody around, thank goodness. The little boy kept saying, "My little sister—my little sister!" I thought that was what he was saying, and I turned around and looked, and there was a little baby who was sinking. I dived out there, got the little baby and brought it up on the bank, turned it over, and proceeded to do artificial respiration on this youngster. This is something I learned in the Boy Scouts. I must have done a good job of learning, because the little baby started crying, and I jumped back into the river.

Above the dam there were several houses of people who worked at the old mill. I got out of the river, and I'm a hollering and screaming and doing my best to get some attention. Finally, this lady, her name was Swain, looked over and asked, "What's going on?"

I said, "I believe you need to call somebody. These people about drowned here. I think maybe you might need to get them some help." She left, and I eased back into the water and waited a minute, and here come the highway patrol down.

So I swam back across to the other side of the dam to get my clothes, which were now wet from the water splashing on them, I guess. I was going to get up and put them on. I bet there were five hundred people down there, and I thought, *What in the world? I've not got a stitch on.* So I got up anyway, put them on, called my dog, and away we went. I got on my bicycle and went home—forgot all about it. The woman ruined my day of fishing.

I then decided I'd go below the Nashville Highway Bridge, below the old armory. Nobody was down there. So my dog and I, we went down there, and I fished the evening away. I got ready to come home, and we went down the old Nashville highway 'til we got to Battleground Drive. I turned up the road, and there were cars everywhere. I thought, *Lordy, what in the world is going on? Something must have happened to my sister.*

My dog and I took off to the house hard as we could to see what it was, and they were looking for me. I asked, "What are you looking for me for? I haven't done anything." Then they told me what I had done was outstanding. To me it didn't mean anything. It had just messed up my day of fishing. This was in August of 1948, and I was sixteen years old.

This incident brought me a lot of notoriety, which I really didn't need, but I did like the money I received in the mail from people. Then I was named American of the Week by Claude Jarman Jr., and I was given a fifty dollar war bond. I thought, *Man, I can buy all sorts of stuff with that and a gold wristwatch;* I don't know what happened to it. It was so fragile that every time something touched it, I'd have to have it worked on.

They said I placed second in the Carnegie Awards and second in the Abbott and Costello Awards. I won American of the Week, which I guess was outstanding. I won the State Safety Award, the Lions Club, the Optimist Club, and Civitan Club awards. You name it, and I won it. But it didn't mean nothing unless it had a few dollars attached to it that I could use to buy more fishing tackle.

I had an interview on WGNS in 1948. It was a very young, nationwide station at the time and Jimmy Fiddler wanted to interview me about what I had done. Well guess what? I forgot about the interview and went fishing. This was a Saturday morning, and here come everybody looking for me on the river. I'd forgot all about going up and talking to Jimmy Fiddler, so they hauled me up there.

For my efforts, the city of Murfreesboro said they would give me a scholarship to go to college. How little did I know that I wouldn't be able to take it. At the time, I wanted to be a veterinarian, but that didn't happen.

To go back a ways, my next-door neighbor had a little girl. In my area, there were probably twenty to twenty-five girls and only four or five boys. This little girl was on the front porch; her name was Faye Spence. We were over there, and she fell into the rain barrel. Well she was drowning, and I pulled her out. The lady who was keeping her came out there and paddled her for falling into the rain barrel. Later in life, I ran into Faye several times. I always thought the world of Faye Spence.

I was in class—I guess it was my sophomore year—after I got those people out of the river, and they called a special meeting with everybody in the study hall. I'm asking everybody, "What are we going to do? What is it?" Didn't anybody know? We got in there, and it was a shock to me they were giving me the State Safety Council award along with several other awards. I don't know whether anybody knew about it, but they certainly didn't tell me.

After I got that woman and children out of the river, I received clippings from about every paper in the United States. From the *Chicago Tribune* to the *New York Sun* or the *New York Times:* you name it, and I got it. I had a big box full. And I got letters from everyone. What did I do? I'd open a letter—didn't read it, but I'd want to see if it had any money in it to buy me more fishing tackle.

At that time, when I was getting all that publicity and they were patting me on the back, I thought, *Gosh, that ain't no big deal! I was just fishing.* It really meant nothing to me. You'd think it would have, but it didn't. The only thing I was interested in was going fishing.

CHAPTER 4

TROUBLESOME TEENS

I managed to survive grammar school and then I started Murfreesboro Central High School. Before I got into high school, there were very few ways you could get to school. Occasionally a school bus would take you, but most of the time they wouldn't. Once you got into high school, the school bus would pick you up.

About the second week of school—why I don't know—I had a pocket full of corn. I guess I was going to start me a cornfield. Well I sat down in my homeroom, and I was looking around and seeing what was going on. And right under my desk was a hole in the floor. I thought, *Well lookie here!* I started putting corn down in that hole. I must have put a double handful down there two or three times. *Ha, put a pencil or two down there, and that would fill it up."* After a while, I thought, I don't guess you can fill it up.

So I scooted my desk over it and settled in to see what was happening. Here comes Homer Pittard. He was the assistant principal at the time. He looked around and asked, "Is there a hole in this corner?"

I said, "I don't see a hole." Well I didn't.

A few minutes later, here comes the biology teacher, Mrs. Charles H. Adkins. (In the old days, most of the teachers went by their husband's name instead of their own last name.) She asked, "Is there anything over here?"

I replied, "Don't see a thing."

Well she left, but about fifteen minutes later, she came back. She jerked my desk out of the way, and there was that hole. She said, "Come with me!" Downstairs I went—two floors down. And guess what? All of that corn and pencils had fallen down into the biology room. She handed me a broom, and in front of all those students, I had to sweep all of that corn up. I had two first cousins in that class, so you can imagine what kind of harassing I got.

As I proceeded through the freshman year, I thought, *You know, I'm going to get even with that woman.* So I got me a smoke bomb. Mrs. Adkins had a little Renault, and I attached it to the spark plugs. And we were all standing out there, waiting on the school bus to come along, when she walked out there and got in it. We all watched as she fired that thing up and it said, "whooo hoooo!" Smoke started boiling out of it. She jumped out and took off running. We got on the school bus and went home.

Mrs. Adkins knew it had to be me, so she talked to me a little bit.

A few days later, she parked her Renault over on the side where the steps were. It just so happened her Renault was parked near the steps at the old Murfreesboro Central. I got four or five young guys like myself, and we picked that thing up and put it up sideways, about four steps up. I went home, and I don't know how she got that thing off the steps. So I got even with Mrs. Charles H. Adkins.

My freshman year at Murfreesboro Central continued up and down. My first-year English teacher was named Mrs. Little. She was a very robust lady, and her husband was a teacher at Middle Tennessee State College. Going into her class one morning, I noticed a roofing tack or a large tack on the floor, so I picked it up. As I walked by her desk, I sat it in her chair, where she would probably sit on it. Or so I thought. I'm sure everybody in there saw me, but nobody said anything.

Mrs. Little came in, and of course everybody was watching—I was too—to see what would happen. She sat down. She didn't even wiggle, and I thought, *Gosh, she's one of those dead-end kids.* Class continued, and when it was over, I started out the door. Then I felt this hand reach out and grab the nape of my neck by the shirt collar. I thought, *Uh-oh!* Mrs. Little grabbed me and said, "Now Mike, the next time you put a tack in my seat, I'm going to throw you down those steps." Well believe it or not, I really believed it. During that first year it seemed like I was always into some kind of trouble.

My homeroom teacher was named Mr. Rogers. He had a Mercury two-door coupe. He thought that car hung the moon. All he would talk about was his Mercury car sitting out there. One day several of us were outside, and we looked around and saw several bales of hay lying around. Being nice, energetic, young men, we gathered all this hay and put it on his Mercury car. When we went back to homeroom, he didn't know who did it. I'm glad he didn't find out.

I went out for football in my freshman year, and Mr. Lee Pate was the coach. I wasn't very good, but I still went. I had to ride a bicycle about a mile and half to two miles every day, back and forth, just to play football. It seemed to me the coach was on my case every day. "Do this. Do that. You haven't done this right." Well I probably hadn't, but it didn't seem like I deserved all this abuse.

They had a smoking shack out beside Murfreesboro Central, and I snuck in there one day; I did smoke a little during the fall. I saw Mr. Pate coming, but he was way down there. I just knew he hadn't seen me, so I hid. Well after practice that afternoon, I started out, and he said, "Mike, give me twenty-five laps around the field for smoking." I thought, *How in the world did that guy see me?* There was nobody on the field but me, running around and around and around that football field. It was dark when I left, and I had to ride my bicycle home. I would estimate I probably lived about four miles from the football stadium, and boy, it was a long, slow ride.

As I progressed through high school—very shakily many of the times—I never had a fatherly figure or anyone to look up to. Mr. Pate became that person. He was on my case more than you can ever believe. It seemed in his opinion, I never did anything right. I had a lot of things to learn, and he was doing a pretty good job of straightening me out. But there was one thing he and everybody else had a hard time doing, and that was keeping me away from the river. That was still my main calling.

On Saturdays while I was a freshman, if I could sneak away before any of the farmers caught me on their property, I would be on the river. I fished both night and day, and needless to say, my mother did not know where I was.

There was an old guy who lived up on the Old Nashville Highway, but he had property on the way to the river, on what they called the Blue Basin. He had truck gardens, and he had everything. He had big vineyards down there, with lots of grapes. When we'd head for the river, we'd have to make a quick stop and load up with grapes, 'cause we figured we wouldn't get any lunch. We'd carry an armload of grapes to the river to eat.

As I went into my junior year of high school, there seemed to be some changes around. Fishing was still number one, but I'll have to admit a lot of these young ladies were beginning to look really, really good to me about this time. I went and got my senior life savings license and proceeded to go to the pool, trying to go to work. Well I wound up working a little at the state park over in Lebanon, Tennessee. This park is known as Cedars of Lebanon State Park. That was a great experience.

In those days, fishing was still very high on my list, but I seemed to have other attractions. I was caught several times sneaking out the back window and out the back door. There were too many places to go and too many things to see; I couldn't stay at home. I guess I was growing up as I progressed through high school, because these events seemed to be further and further apart, but they still happened on occasion.

I played football, basketball, and softball in high school, and we had a pool outside the building. During recreation, if you wanted to, you could go swimming. Well that was one thing I was pretty proficient at.

And those were my high school years.

CHAPTER 5

FAMILY

M y mother and father both grew up within ten miles of the city of Murfreesboro. In those days, education was not such a great thing to have. My mother had a small amount of education—I think the third grade—and my father went maybe to the fifth grade. My father's name was Hershel M. Lorance, and my mother was Martha Pearl Watson.

My mother and father both came from big families; that's the way it was back in those old days. They had big families to take care of the farm. For many years, the main employment company in Murfreesboro was the Carnation Milk company. That's where my father retired from after over forty years. My mother retired from the Veterans Administration Hospital after about thirty years.

My mother worked hard and did the best she could. She was like a lot of people back in those olden days. She didn't have a lot of education, but she managed to raise two kids on her own.

I've been asked where I got the will to do the things I do. I guess it was instilled in me many, many years ago, when my mother and father got a divorce, and I was sort of left on my own. It's not easy out there when you don't have a big brother to guide you along the way. I had a sister, but if I did anything wrong, she was always trying to help me. Yeah, help me get a spanking. But I guarantee you that if I did get into trouble, she would be there to help me out.

When I was growing up, you had to fend for yourself. You had to work, and you had to do whatever was necessary. I had nobody to give me money, the way the children do now. I had to work for everything I got, and my mother didn't have a lot of extras.

I had two main influences, I guess, in my life at that time. One was my football coach, Lee Pate, and the other one was my stepfather, James Shipp. I was about seventeen years old when my mother married James. He was a really good person. I don't know how he put up with me and the things that were happening, but he did. He also helped get me through some really rough times. I used to think Lee Pate mistreated me out on the football field, and I later told him that, but he really didn't. He was trying to help straighten me out, and I guess he might have done a pretty good job.

There were a lot of incidental things that happened as I progressed through life. I was going out with this nice young lady, and I went to pick her up one night—I had already gone out with her sister—and here comes this young lady through there, and she looked really good. I said "Huh, who are you?" She gave me her name, and I couldn't remember it. I told her, "I'll see you later."

She replied, "I hope not."

Later I did call and said, "I would like to speak to Ruth."

"No Ruth in this house."

"Well is there anybody there with a name that begins with an R?"

"Yeah, there's Ruby."

"I'd like to speak to her." So I spoke to her, and guess what? We had a date, and away we went. By the way, her name was Ruby Smotherman.

I told Ruby, "You know what? If you'd get you a job, I think we'd get married." Well guess what? She got her a job with State Farm in Nashville, and I spent many a night, riding back and forth from Nashville to Murfreesboro. As things may have it, I asked her to marry me, and she said she would. I asked, "What day would you like to get married on?"

She said, "Thanksgiving Day, because I'm off on Friday, Saturday, and Sunday."

I said, "I can't get married on Thanksgiving Day."

"Why not?"

"That's the day rabbit season opens, and I go rabbit hunting every Thanksgiving Day."

So we got married on November 26, 1954, and that was probably one of the most important days of my life. We moved into an apartment and got settled down. Things were doing quite well until October 10, 1955.

Then came that little bundle of joy everybody's looking for. Patricia Ann Lorance was born that particular day, October 10, 1955. When they brought her out, everybody was excited and said, "Oh, how pretty she is!" But when I saw she was red and all wrinkled, I thought, *Surely that's not what my wife and I came up with.* That was the ugliest baby I believe I ever saw. I will have to say that after a short time, she really became a quite nice-looking little girl.

She didn't realize it wouldn't be long before I wouldn't be able to see what she looked like or know how she was acting when she was doing things she wasn't supposed to do. But as she got a little older, she got a little smarter. She could figure out how to do things so I couldn't catch her at it.

To show you how much I really thought of fishing, the day before my wife and I greeted the birth of our child, we were fishing on Todd's Lake. The next night we went to the movie, and we left the movie and went to the hospital. That changed a lot of things.

My sister and I both lost our vision in our late twenties due to a particular genetic disease. It's a degeneration of the retina, and both parents have to have the gene that causes the problem. The mother passes it to the daughter, and the father passes it to the son, or so I have been told.

When my sister, Georgia Mai, got old enough and out of high school, she decided she wanted to be a nurse. Georgia's nursing school was Baptist General in Nashville, where she went for four years. She would have been a registered nurse, but the last six months of her schooling, her eyes would not permit her to do the surgical work that was necessary for her to complete her degree.

Georgia Mai lives in Littleton, Colorado, and Ruby and I went to visit them one time. We went up in the Rockies, and I decided I was going to ride a snow lift up. I didn't know what that thing did, but on it I got. The snow lift was in Berthoud Pass. Well I had a little jacket on; it was in June and wasn't so cold. Ruby and I got up on top of that mountain, and I liked to have frozen. And when you want to get off of that thing, it stops, and you got to hop off. Me? I didn't know what was in front of me, but I hopped off, and snow was ankle deep. I could hardly wait to get that thing turned around and head back down the hill. We got back down the hill and guess what? Ruby hid behind a sign and started a snowball battle. Boy, she got the worst end of that. We pelted her with snowballs!

CHAPTER 6

RUBY

Permission has been granted to include the following column along with Mike's story. It was published March 23, 2006, in the *Daily News Journal* in Murfreesboro. It was authored by Greg Pogue, who is executive sports editor of the DNJ and editor of this book.

If eyes are gateways to the heart, then those of Ruby Lorance had to have been blood red for many of years.

She passed away Tuesday. They're burying her tonight. Her love for those around her, especially husband, Mike, will endure forever.

For decades, Ruby Lorance not only lived life for herself, but saw everything for her husband as well, whose blindness that would have crippled many a man was nothing but a hindrance along the way to living life to the brim.

Or maybe that should be bream, as in fish dangling from the hook. Mike Lorance sure has caught plenty of fish, many keepers and more thrown back, even when the magnitude of the haul was trophy size for most.

Fifty-one years they were married. The preacher who performed their wedding in 1954 at Third Baptist Church will offer the eulogy tonight that can only write itself.

"Not many people will devote their time to the way she helped other people," Mike says of wife Ruby, a pioneer in the insurance business with State Farm who retired from the Murfreesboro-based operation in 1996, after 43 years of service.

Nor will many live their life as a spouse of the blind. Then again, not many could distinguish fishing lures and line weights for a well-respected angler who's been the outdoors columnist of the *Daily News Journal* for more than two decades.

When Mike Lorance eventually went blind eight years into their marriage because of retina degeneration, it only began a recommitment to the other that stood the test of time. Then again, how proud Ruby was the day in 1980 when her husband became the only blind person to ever compete professionally on the BASS (Bass Anglers Sportsman Society) circuit.

"It is tough when you live with somebody who is blind," Mike says. "It is a sighted world. And you just have to adjust. I know it was a constant struggle."

It didn't stop the couple from living, though. Often, trips to the Caribbean would include hauling sailfish and tuna into the boat. And as her husband's national notoriety grew, Ruby relished in it every step of the way. Fishing was always good for the Lorances, even when they weren't biting.

But Ruby Lorance also took pride in raising a family, especially daughter Patricia and grandchildren Brian, Dustin, JJ, Craig and Chris.

"She was my eyes and my friend and my loving wife," says Mike, noting in recent years Ruby had been a primary caregiver to her mother, sister, mother-in-law and father-in-law. "She was always meaning so much to so many people. She was such a caring and compassionate person."

How ironic Ruby's smiling photo ran with her obituary Wednesday in the *Daily News Journal,* the same week her husband's mug shot will not. Somehow today's edition of the DNJ feels less than full without Mike's outdoors column gracing it.

Oh, it will be back next week. And Mike will tell us again which fishing hole is yielding what or, better yet, which buddy has fallen from the boat or run out of gas in the middle of the lake.

When he does, think of Ruby. I know Mike will be.

Ruby as Mike remembers her

As others remember her

CHAPTER 7

LADDIE

I found this little dog and named her Lulu. She was a pretty little shepherd, and she and I really got to be friends in a hurry. Well she had some puppies. She met me at the school bus every day. One day I came in from school, and she was so excited to see me she ran into the road. A car hit and killed her. I was very devastated. I went home. I guess you'd have to say I cried a lot, and I looked at her little puppies. I raised the puppies and kept one of them—it was a yellow one. That yellow shepherd followed me everywhere. I went and named him Laddie.

He ran loose, like they did in those days. When I was fifteen or sixteen, I had some neighbors who said they saw a dog come through there with his mouth foaming. In those days, if you thought a dog had rabies, they killed every dog in the area. Well they came to my house. They said, "We come to kill your dog."

I said, "No you haven't. First person that shoots my dog, I'm going to shoot him. I'll put my dog up, but nobody's going to shoot my dog."

George Franklin was one of the guys who was going to shoot my dog. But guess what? My dog never was shot. They later found out somebody had fed the dog that came through some glass, and that's why his mouth was foaming.

When my mother would spank me, she'd have to take me inside the house and shut the door, because the old, yellow shepherd wouldn't allow it. There were times when I would try to slip off from him and go to the river and not let him know I was going. I wouldn't see him around, and I'd be going. And about the time I'd get close to the riverbank, I'd look around, and he'd be bouncing along beside me. He'd been watching all the time for me to take off, so he could sneak in behind me.

When you're young and swimming in the river, people would come along, find your clothes on the riverbank, and tie them in knots. In all those years, I never had my clothes tied. Everybody else would have knotted clothes, but not me. The old dog was lying there, and you wouldn't dare touch one of my garments.

Above the dam where I got those people out of the river, we both would swim. I'd dive off and swim, and here he'd come. He'd have to swim, too. The day I got the people out, I don't think Laddie swam the river. I never looked around to see, but he was there with my clothes when I got back.

CHAPTER 8

FORT LOST IN THE WOODS

I turned eighteen, and I don't know how in the world I did, but I managed to get out of high school. I guess most of my problems were behind me. It didn't take me long after I got out of high school to decide I needed a job. Things outside were not any better than they were before I graduated; you had to work to get anything. I tried for a job at the service station at Seward Air Force Base (in Smyrna) and went to work when I was out of school about three or four weeks. I went to work for this base service station for the humongous sum of seventy-five cents an hour, which to me was an awful lot of money, since I didn't have very much.

I was progressing rather rapidly in the service station business, and I thought, *Man, this is all right!* I worked there until I was about nineteen. I had purchased a car and was doing quite well. Then came the note from the federal government.

It said, "Your friends and neighbors have selected you to be drafted into the service." I thought, *Man, I'd like to meet some of those friends and neighbors.* I was drafted into the combat engineers and sent to Fort Jackson, South Carolina, and then to Fort Leonard Wood, Missouri.

I was nineteen years old, and away I went from home for my first time. Let me tell you, this was an experience! The military transported me to Nashville, and I thought, *Ach! I will get to go home and get all my clothes.* Well guess what? We left Nashville that night and went to Fort Jackson, South Carolina.

When you're away from home the first time, you don't really know what to do. In Fort Jackson, they put us down in "tent city." That night it was cold—it was in January—and we were in tents! The bottom part of the tent was wood, and the upper part was canvas. We had a little coal stove in the middle of the tent, and there was about eight of us in there. Everything would be rocking right along, really nice, until the middle of the night. Then the stovepipe would stop up, and smoke would fill the tent. Somebody had to clean the pipe.

They gave us one blanket. Wind would come in one side of the tent, go under the blanket, and out the other side of the tent. I'm telling you those were some miserable nights. You'd get up in the morning, and the ground would be frozen, and by ten o'clock, it would be hot as a firecracker.

They sent us from Fort Jackson to Fort Leonard Wood, Missouri. We called it "Fort Lost in the Woods." There were only eight of us who made this trip halfway across the country. I stopped in Memphis broker than a church mouse; didn't have a quarter. I called home and got them to send me some money by Western Union, and boy was I ready to go then. Off to Fort Leonard Wood we went.

Well the first part was great! We all had this big meeting, and we went around; they showed us a lot of things. They gave us our barracks and they said, "Now boys, Friday night we are going to have a party." I thought, *Man, this is great! I've been in service for one week and we're going to have a party!* Here comes Friday night, and everybody was all excited. Guess what the party was? We had scrub brushes, soap, and buckets, and we had to scrub the floor. That was the sorriest party I ever attended.

We were in the combat engineers, and we were there before the next cycle started. That is when you go through your basic training, so guess what? They had us out in the woods, cutting down timber. It was exciting, too, because every now and then, a tank would come through. You had better have all your stuff together so you could run, because that thing didn't wait for nobody.

They come around with our dinner while we were there—they had it in garbage cans. They had big old garbage cans of pinto beans or whatever else they had, and they would tell you, "Keep your mess kit and gear clean." Well you had one mess; it was a knife, fork, and spoon. After you finished your lunch, supper, or whatever you were eating, there were big garbage cans where you washed your mess gear. We'd better get it clean, because if we didn't, the next day there would be guys all out under the bushes—they had what you'd call the GIs. Very fortunately, I grew up keeping all these things clean, and I never got sick one day. But man, there were some poor guys up under the trees.

As we progressed through basic, a lot of things happened. They taught you all these deals about how you use a bayonet. You make all kinds of racket; you hit him with the butt of the stock and then stick him with the knife. Wasn't that great?

We went to the firing range. Everybody was lined up and down the firing range. I don't know how many—there were two or three hundred. Then you'd start shooting. They had these targets that started at three hundred and five hundred yards. They had guys down there pulling targets. If someone missed the target, they had what they called "Maggie Drawers." They waved it back and forth. In other words, you better hit the target!

Then it came my time to be in the trench, pulling the target. You pull the target down, mark where the guy hit it, and raise it back up. If he missed, you would wave Maggie Drawers. When it was our turn to pull the targets, the sergeant said, "If everybody doesn't qualify, we all got to come back on Saturday morning."

Well the guys who were shooting—no wonder we had so many of our own men hit; these guys couldn't hit the courthouse. They'd shoot at the target next to them or the one that was above them; it didn't make any difference. You'd pull that thing down that had no marks, and since you didn't want to come back out here on Saturday—you'd punch a hole in it and raise it. Man, he'd hit close to the bull's-eye! They'd have missed the target or hit three or four targets down. But guess what? Everybody qualified!

Then the cadre would get us out on the parade ground on Saturday morning, preparing to give us the day off. You'd go down there, and they'd say left right, left right. And if you missed and went right when you were supposed to go left, they'd give you a rock to carry. Well it wasn't long until I had two rocks; one in each hand. Didn't know my left from my right. They'd stutter and stammer, and you couldn't keep up with what they were saying. They'd do it on purpose!

After they got through with the parade, they said, "Everybody can go in!" Well if you went in and stretched out on your bunk, guess what? They had duties for you to do. It didn't take long for us to decide when we had any free time we should slip out the window, run out the door, and get away quickly. Otherwise, they'd maybe have you cleaning out the grease pit or doing whatever else they could come up with for you to do. We'd all run over to the PX or the USO office building, where you could get a little nap in the big, soft chairs.

Fort Leonard Wood was where I found out my future didn't look too great. The doctors reported to me that my eyes were going bad, and they were going to have to discharge me from the service. To make matters worse, I had just passed the test to be admitted into officer candidate school (OCS). That went out the window, too.

I hated being discharged, because I liked what I was doing. I rather enjoyed all this going back and forth and doing all the things they wanted us to do. But I was discharged and came back to the great city of Murfreesboro. So that wound up my military career.

When I got back from service and went back to work at the base service station, I met a lot of people. There was Ariba Jill, a lieutenant nurse over in the hospital. We became quite friendly. Another tragedy arrived in my life. She was flying in a plane over New York in one of the old C-119s. It crashed, and she was killed.

Another friend of mine was named Major Withers. We were in Murfreesboro one day, and he and I matched for a drink in a restaurant. But I lost, so I bought him a 7UP. He left that day, and over Idaho, his C-119 also crashed, and he was killed.

CHAPTER 9

FINDING WORK

After my stint in the army and was back at work at the service station, I was thinking, *You know, I'd like to do something else, but I don't really know what I want to do.* Then I happened to remember the city of Murfreesboro had told me they would give me a scholarship for getting those people out of the river. *Now is a good time to take it!* I went out to Middle Tennessee and started taking the test to get in. I noticed I was having a lot of problems seeing. *This is not going to work. I don't think I can read all these papers that they've got out here. I don't think I can do it.* So I decided to do something else.

I decided I would like to work in the tire business, so I went to work for Wade Williams. I worked for him for quite a while and then went to Jennings Tire Company. While at Jennings Tire Company, they asked me to take over a service station at Lamb's Truck Stop. Well this was a little more down my line. While I was there, I got this offer from George Franklin to open up a new service station down the road from where I was. So I took that job.

Another gentleman wanted me to help him. I stayed there for a year or so and then this guy wanted me to run his car lot, which was a big challenge. I had to sell the cars and trade for whatever was being turned in. Somebody made out the papers for me. There's one thing that you learn when you're dealing with people like this: you have to be really,

really careful. I had learned enough about automobiles that it was hard to fool me. I knew what to look for in case there was something wrong with the vehicle—if it was the transmission, I knew how to look for it, or the rear end or whatever the case may be. So there were very few times I had very many close calls. When I'd sell a car, the lady would fill out the papers, and the customer would be on his or her merry way. The customer would never even know I was blind.

During this time, there were several car lots in Murfreesboro that wanted me to work for them. I worked for Broadway Motors, Charlie Thomas's car lot Five Day Motors—that's where I stayed for two or three years—and was very successful and managed to at least have money to buy things.

My wife had someone walk up to her one time and say, "Your husband is a really good car salesman, but he needs to put that bottle down. I think he's a little drunk." The truth be known, I didn't even drink! But sometimes it's hard to conceal being blind. You might run into something, and people would think you are out on a drinking binge. Even after all these years since I sold automobiles, I still occasionally have someone come up to me and tell me they purchased a car from me, and they did not know I was blind. To me, that's great! I'm always glad to hear something like that—at least they're not buying the car because they think I'm blind.

During this time, my wife, Ruby, was the one who really held us together. I had a hard, hard time, and I'm sure I made it hard on her, but she stuck with me. She's got to have stars in her crown, because I don't imagine she got any from me. These were some really dark times, and I didn't do much to help enlighten people around me, I'm sure. I probably had an attitude, because I didn't know what to do. Then in 1962, I was declared blind. That was a long time ago.

One day I asked myself, *What am I going to do? I can't continue in this way.* So I contacted people in Nashville and decided I wanted to open a sporting goods store. Well that's exactly what I did. I opened Mike's Sport Shop in 1968.

I stayed there for about six or seven years. Can you imagine a blind guy running a sport goods store? What does he know about guns? What does he know about fishing equipment or archery equipment? Well the truth be known, I knew quite a bit about all of them. I sold guns, fishing tackle, and archery equipment—just about anything I could think of that might catch the interest of people coming into the store.

The stresses of being blind caused a lot of problems. Problems: I had more of those you could count with an adding machine. I lost my faith in mankind when I owned that store. Friends—at least those you thought were friends—pocketed your stuff; they thought I didn't know, but I did. I wouldn't say anything, but I'd think, *Well I guess you need it worse than I do,* and I'd let them go out the door.

While I was in the sporting goods business, I got into another business. I decided I would like to have a radio show, maybe to help promote my business. Can you imagine a blind guy with a sporting goods store having a radio show? Well that's what I did. Hardly anyone listening to the show knew I was blind, and I didn't go out to tell them, because I figured if I told them, they wouldn't be listening any more.

I grew up on what was Battleground Drive, and I used to hunt all the area out there, including where all the shopping centers are. Where the main road goes through those are all my old hunting grounds. And when I went to school, I had to cut across there to walk to school. When I was in the shopping center in Mike's Sport Shop, I used to walk up the street and think, *Boy, I've walked this place a many a time hunting day and night when I could see.*

When I opened this shop, I knew nothing about what I really needed. So I started looking around. I met this gentleman named James Smith. He was a factory representative for several gun lines and fishing equipment. I asked him what I had to do to buy merchandise directly from him, which would be almost directly from the factory. He was impressed by a blind guy trying to open a shop and said, "We normally reserve that for people with a lot of money, but in your case, we are going to give you the opportunity." I purchased Franchi shotguns, Mannlicher rifles, and a variety of lures from James Smith. James was one of the nicest gentlemen I ever met, and what he did for me was really great. I became the largest Franchi shotgun retail outlet in the southeastern United States, and that's pretty good for a small shop in a small shopping center. I sold Franchi shotguns to everyone I could think of.

One day this IBM employee, who worked on machines at State Farm Insurance Companies, came into the store and wanted to buy a shotgun. I sold him a little twenty-gauge Franchi. The gun only weighed five and a half pounds, and that meant it would kick. The gentleman's name was Ray Pierson, and he had two other guys with him. One of them was Ralph Gannon, and the other one was Dillard Parsley. These guys were going dove hunting.

In about three or four days, all three gentlemen came back to see me. The first thing Ray said to me was, "Mike, there's something wrong with this shotgun!"

"Ray, what in the world is the matter?"

"It is double firing."

"Ray, that is impossible. It's an automatic, and it's not going to double fire—it's not a fully automatic shotgun."

"Every time I shot this gun, there were two shells on the ground."

"I don't know how that could happen." So I told Dillard and Ralph, "You boys go back, and y'all watch him. Let me know what's happening."

A few days later, the gentlemen came into the store, and they were all sort of laughing. I said, "Okay guys, what's happening?" Dillard and Ralph both agreed that every time Ray pulled the trigger on the shotgun, he closed his eyes and pulled the trigger again. He didn't even realize it, but he was shooting the gun twice, because it would kick so hard. I told him, "Ray, if the gun's kicking that hard, I'll try to find you something else that you won't have to worry about kicking so hard." But he didn't want to sell it.

I also started a fishing club. We met in the basement of this shopping center my store was in, and we formed a fishing league. We had tournaments and all sorts of things that brought a lot of enjoyment to family anglers. But like everything that's got competition involved—at that time, at least—it evolved and became more of a fishing tournament for men than it did for families.

Besides those who came into the shop with sticky fingers, my biggest problem with the store was where it was located. It was located on the bottom floor at the back of a strip mall. There were a lot of break-ins. Thieves made a swinging door out of my front door. I had two alarm systems set up, and they couldn't even catch me, I don't believe.

I had a row of guns up there, and this gentleman down the hall had purchased one from me. He said, "I'll pick it up at the first of the month."

I said, "Okay."

Before he came in to get it, thieves broke into the store and got a lot of guns. He came running in. "Did they get the gun? Did they get the gun?"

I said, "No, that's the only one they left."

He said, "Good gracious! I really didn't want it!" But guess what? He was stuck with the firearm.

I met a lot of great people while I had Mike's Sport Shop in Jackson Heights Shopping Center, and I still run into a lot of those people who remember when the store was there and really miss it. I had many different guns there, and I traded a lot of guns. I'm sure there were also some people who thought, and I'm sure said many times, "We'll go down there and take advantage of that guy. He can't see." Well guess what? That happened so seldom I can't even remember when it did happen. I usually came out on the long end of the deal.

During the seventies and eighties, there was very little information going out over the radio to hunters and fishermen in our area. So I decided I would try to start a hunting and fishing show and launched the program on WMTS radio station in Murfreesboro. I had a program every Friday, and it was sponsored, which at that time was hard to come by. What I did was try to get everybody's name in there that I could. That way, I would hopefully have more business in the store.

On the program I kept fishermen up to date on where the fish were being taken, what they were being taken on, and in most cases, who was catching the fish and the lures they were using. You could not always depend on them telling you what lures they were catching the fish on, but we would sort of figure it out.

During the hunting segment of the show, we would talk about where the game was being harvested in what area of the county or state, and what kind of license was required to hunt those particular animals. I also had guys on who were killing the big deer or whatever they were doing—rabbit hunting, quail hunting, squirrel hunting, or whatever pertained to the outdoors. I would have their name and where they were hunting.

I had lots of connections with many of the people who produced fishing equipment—fishing lures, rods, reels. Whenever a new innovation came out, I would be one of the first to have it on the radio to pass it out among the fishermen.

My radio show was one of the longest-running radio shows in middle Tennessee for many years. The thing I enjoyed most about doing the radio show was that I got involved with a lot of people. When I would have something on there that helped them, and they told me it did, it really made me feel good. We didn't think the show would last very long, but it was successful for fifteen years. I am proud I was able to do this. After all these years, people still ask me, "When are you going back on the air with a television or radio show?" That always makes me feel good to know people were listening or watching and still remember.

CHAPTER 10

THE CABIN

For several years we rocked along, and everything was doing well. In the late fifties, though, there suddenly came a change. That's when my eyesight started going from bad to worse. I couldn't see very well, and I was having a hard time holding a job. I really didn't know what to do. Have you ever heard of desperation? Well that's exactly what it was. I was desperate.

After a while I guess I readjusted, and my wife, Ruby, was a mainstay. She would not allow me any self-pity or depression. She said, "Decide what you wanted to do and then go on and do it!" Ruby was working at State Farm and going up the ladder of success. Several things can be said about Ruby, but the most important is that she was determined. She was willing to work and didn't back away from any job.

During this time, she pushed me at every opportunity, or so she said. Or maybe she did, and I just didn't realize it. But in the years that followed, I learned she had done quite a job of preparing me for the future. Whatever I attempted after I went blind, she stood behind me, regardless of what it was. When I opened Mike's Sport Shop, she was behind me. She would help me in any way she could.

During this period, Ruby was moving into management at State Farm. She helped establish several departments. One was the multi-payment department, and apparently she did a good job, because she was asked to apply for the position of the new micrographics department, which was where everything was put on microfilm. In addition to supervising the micrographics department she was also to supervise the word-processing department.

Ruby progressed quite well. When State Farm Credit Union got its first million she was this department's supervisor.

I can remember a rather funny instance. We were at a State Farm anniversary supper, sitting at a table with the regional vice president and some of the other influential people at State Farm. After the dinner, a lady dancer was performing. She was dancing, and she went over to this elderly gentleman, who was a former regional vice president at State Farm. He couldn't hear, and she tried to get him up and to dance, but he didn't understand what was going on. That was a hoot!

The next thing I knew, there was an arm reaching for me. I thought, *What in the world?* I reached out to see what it was, and she had all kinds of bracelets on her arm. I said, "I don't know this lady, but it looks like she wants me to go somewhere." So up I went. We got up in front of the State Farm audience, and though a lot of them couldn't see us, we brought down the house. She didn't know I was blind, so she just turned me loose. And there I was in the middle of the floor and didn't know where to go.

Then a hand reached out and got me and led me to the side. I found out later it was one of the top management people who had helped me off the floor. The superintendent of Ruby's department said, "Ye gads! She has picked two of the worst people in the whole audience. One can't hear and the other one can't see!"

After the dinner was over and we were going out, everybody was asking, "What was going on? What was going on?" Well we really put some light in that particular anniversary supper.

My wife and I were beginning to get straightened out, and things were a whole lot better than they had been in some previous times. We were able to go on vacations and do other things everybody else got to do. For a long time we had been sort of straddled with bills and things that we couldn't do anything about.

I was still fishing every chance I got, but there was one thing I always did. I reserved Friday night to take my wife out to wherever she wanted to go. The rest of the time was open to fishing. The only time I didn't do this was if I had a tournament. Then I would fish the tournament, but we would go out some other night.

In 1977 Ruby and I bought some lots on Center Hill Lake. We couldn't decide what we wanted to do, so we moved a house trailer onto the two lots. That little fellow looked as ugly as an old white shoe. I had a guy come in and level my lot up, and I didn't stay up there while he did the work. He brought one end down lower than the other, and the trailer looked like an airplane getting ready to take off. It was definitely ugly.

Clyde Craddock has some property right above me, and he said, "You know, I've got a lot up on this hill up here, and it's got water and everything. I'd be glad to trade with you."

I said, "No, I don't think I want to trade. I'll just keep what I have." Clyde had decided that ugly trailer was going to make everybody unhappy, but he didn't really know what was about to happen.

Ruby, with her ambition, started painting this trailer, and it really looked good. Then we built a deck on it. We cut the end out of it and put in sliding doors. When we got through, it really didn't look like the ugly trailer it was when we first got there.

Then the lady we bought the first two lots from said she had four more she'd like to sell us, so we bought those. We had lots that ran all the way to the high water mark, which is about as close as anybody in the country can get on Center Hill Lake.

We kept that trailer for several years. Then we built what I believe is one of the sorriest cabins you could build. It was an A-frame. We wanted a chalet, but I guess we were too dumb to tell the difference between an A-frame and a chalet. That A-frame is good for one thing, but I don't know what it is. You can't put your furniture next to the wall, you can't heat it, and you can't cool it. Beams ran from the ceiling to the floor, and if you weren't careful when you went behind the bed or did something else, you would bang your head on the rafters.

We built a big deck on the front and a deck on the rear, and we had a really nice little summer cabin. This little A-frame had about a thousand to eleven hundred feet in it, which was plenty of room for a vacation home, but it sure was tough to arrange your furniture when the roof came almost all the way down to the ground.

I stayed up at that cabin several times by myself, including a week with just me and my dog. My guide dog was named Gina, and we went down to the lake and fished, went up and down the bank, and did everything anybody else would do. We'd come in and cook supper and then we'd go out on the deck and sort of relax, "watching" the sun go down and listening to the water hit the bank. That was a pretty nice time. Though I couldn't see the sun, I could tell it was going down. But at the end of the week, I was really ready to come home. I was tired of cooking and cleaning and wandering all over the cabin by myself. I needed a little company, and Ruby was that company.

I fished Center Hill so much that everybody up there got to know me. I mean I fished it day and night. I told Ruby one time, "What we need to do is to build us a little motel on those four lots down there and then we could come up here and stay a lot longer."

She said, "That's out!"

I asked, "Why would that be out?"

She said, "You'd build the cabins, and I'd have to take care of them, because you'd be gone fishing."

Ruby and I would come up on the weekend, and I would go down and fish a lot of times off the bank. She would either walk down with me to start with or drop me off from the vehicle, and I'd fish. I tell her when I'd want her to come back, and she'd come back and pick me up.

One day I told her to come back and get me about twelve o'clock. Well I was ready to come home earlier than that, so I took off, and up the hill I went to the cabin. In the meantime, Ruby came looking for me. She went to where I was, and I wasn't there! She came back up and asked a man standing there, "Have you seen a blind guy go by here?"

He was taken aback and then answered, "No, ma'am, I sure have not." Ruby thought about how she sounded and laughed. She quickly made her way up the bank to the cabin and found me there. Since then, we've had quite a few laughs when we shared this incident with other people.

On the weekends I could, I would fish Center Hill at night with a lot of the guys I fished with up there. When we got through fishing, they'd let me off at the ramp, and I'd walk up to the cabin. Sometimes it would be two or three o'clock in the morning, and I'd go in the back door and sneak into bed. Ruby often didn't even know when I came in.

Considering the trials and tribulations I put her through, my wife had to be a very forgiving person. A lot of times I would go fishing and forget to tell her. Well that brought on a little talk. People used to ask her, "Don't you worry about Mike going fishing?"

"If I haven't heard from him in two or three days, then I might start worrying."

There were a lot of tournaments held out of Sligo Boat Dock when we had the cabin up there, and there were a lot of times I came in with cash I had won on some of the pot tournaments. Word got around that you had to watch out for me and the guy I was fishing with, or we might take your money up there. It was really great to have people think I'm a good fisherman when, in reality, I might think, *Well, I'm not really very good,* but they think so.

As I grew older I leaned on Ruby quite a bit more than I probably should have. But she was willing to do whatever was necessary to promote the things I wanted to do. Ruby worked at State Farm for forty-three years, and when she retired, I'm sure there was a void left. There was no "backup" for Ruby—whenever there was something that needed to be done, she would do it, and I'm sure that after she retired, the people at State Farm really missed the things she did for everyone.

In the seventies, Dot Matthews, her husband, Don, and her sister Shirley Putman, Ruby, and I would go to Lake Eufaula in Alabama. That was usually around my birthday, which was April 10. You cannot believe the number of fish we caught during that time. We usually brought back enough for quite a few fish suppers for many weeks.

Many times Ruby, Trish, and I would go down, and I would take my guide dog. Most of those guys knew me by that time, and there was always somebody that wanted to take me out fishing. So I had an outstanding time on Lake Eufaula and caught an awful lot of fish.

Being blind is not the greatest thing when you're traveling a lot. You don't see anything! I like to travel, but I like it better when we get there. We had a television in the van, but it wouldn't play. And the radio wouldn't play in a lot of areas. So that made riding down the road a little boring.

Ruby and I and some of her friends and some of my friends were always going on vacation somewhere. We went to Florida, and I said, "I think I want to go out deep sea fishing!" So we went over and met the captain on the boat. We talked to him a little while, and I said, "I think I'll go out with you tomorrow."

Well the next thing I knew, he's talking to my wife. He asked her, "How can he fish? He's blind! What do I do?"

She said, "Well you just get him aboard and turn him loose. Everything will be all right."

When we came in the next afternoon, he went up to Ruby and said, "He caught all the fish! I thought I'd tell the rest of these people that if you blindfold yourself, you'd probably catch a lot more fish." He also told her he'd be glad to take me out anytime I wanted to go. I thought that was great!

Ruby told me one time, "You shouldn't tell these people you're blind unless they ask." But you feel a little guilty when you don't, and when you do tell them, they feel a little guilty. She'd always make sure I had my clothes arranged properly and looked halfway decent. She said, "You are a representative of blind people as well as a representative of me, so if you look bad, it looks bad on me as well as other blind people."

We went to this big rib place in Nashville one night. There were four of us: Dot Matthews, her husband, Don, Ruby, and myself. There was no place to park. Ruby commented the only thing left was the handicapped spot, so I said, "Ruby, pull into the handicapped spot."

She said, "Nobody is handicapped." I said, "I think I am!"

So she pulled in and said, "Meet me at the back." So I got out and went around the back to meet her. "Act like you're blind! They'll be over here and arresting us!" For years I had tried to act like I'm not blind, so people would appreciate whatever it was I did. And there she was, trying to get me to act like I was blind to keep her from getting a ticket. I'm sure if I had wanted a handicap sticker I could have gotten one, but I didn't really believe I needed one. I could get around and do the things I wanted to do without having a handicap sticker.

For a time after I got my guide dog I had quite a lot of trouble eating out. We'd go to a restaurant and think we could sit down, and someone would say, "Nah, you can't come in here with that dog. That's not allowed."

I'd say, "Well it's a guide dog," and I'd show them my card.

I'd get a firm, "I don't care. You gotta go." I got run out of more places than Joe Louis got hit.

Upstairs from Mike's Sport Shop and down the avenue just a short way was a pizza parlor. One night I was late closing the store, and I told my wife we'd go down there and have supper. Well my wife, daughter, my dog, who had on a guide dog harness, and I went in and sat down. My dog was much too big by this time; she got up to ninety-eight pounds. She was a pretty healthy young dog.

The lady came over and took our order. She left but came back and said, "I'm sorry, sir. You'll have to take the dog out."

I said, "I'm sorry, too, but I'm not taking her anywhere. This is a guide dog, and I came to have dinner tonight, and that's exactly what we're going to have. I'd like to see the manager." This incident was the first time I sort of bucked up and decided, "This is far enough. I've been kicked around enough, and this is not going to happen anymore."

The waitress was gone probably twenty or thirty minutes, and I was fuming. My wife said, "Let's go. Let's go. Let's go."

I said, "Nope, I am not going anywhere. I'm going to stay right here."

The waitress finally returned. "The manager said to take your order." Well that cured that problem, but there were a lot of other problems I had to cure.

Chapter 11

Seeing Eye

After I was given the news that I was going blind, I had about a year or two when I could see a little and was still fishing. The problem with my eyes is I lost my central vision first. I've got retinitis stigmatosis, a degeneration of the retina. If you start losing your vision from your nose out, you lose your central vision. If you're fortunate enough to start losing from the outside in, you'll lose your peripheral vision. With your central vision, you'll still be able to see, maybe for quite a long while. But as it was, that didn't work with me. It wasn't too many months before I was just about out of business.

To give you an idea of how much I liked to drive and places I wanted to go, I have driven when I could see cars, but I couldn't tell a lot about them before I'd pull out on the street. In those days, there were very few cars, not like it is now. If that were to happen now, I wouldn't make it to the front door. But I'd start out, and I'd look and then I'd listen. If I didn't hear anything, then I'd go. That's how dumb you can be when you really want to do something.

In 1962 I was declared blind. I drove home one day, pulled the car in the front yard, got out, and petted it. "This is your last trip," I told the car. "I won't be driving you anymore."

I told Ruby I was blind and couldn't drive anymore, and it sort of took her aback. "What are we going to do?" I had no idea what I was going to do, but I knew I had to do something. I couldn't go through life without working.

Finally, I decided there was something I needed to do that I was not doing. So I contacted the Lions Club in Murfreesboro, in which Tommy Martin was very prominent at that time. We all had a meeting, and Tommy and the others said, "You need to go to Little Rock, Arkansas, to learn to use a cane and how to eat and do other things." I thought, *No, I can learn to eat by myself. And I don't want a cane, because it's too slow.* In the previous chapter I mentioned my guide dog. Well, this is when I decided that a guide dog was the way to go.

I told this group what I wanted was a dog, and they all tried to discourage me from doing it. They wanted me to go around with a cane. Well that wasn't my style. So I contacted Seeing Eye, which is in Morristown, New Jersey. For those who don't know, Seeing Eye, where I have gotten my guide dogs since 1968, was started in Nashville, Tennessee, in 1929. They stayed there until 1938, but due to the heat and lack of contributions to this program, they moved to Morristown, New Jersey.

They were the first guide dog school in the United States. The first person to have a guide dog, or a dog guide, was a guy named Morris Frank. He was a graduate of Vanderbilt University and had an insurance business in Nashville. He did things with guide dogs that really, really made me want to have one from Seeing Eye.

I contacted Seeing Eye, which is not supported by anything other than donations from the public. The federal government or state government has nothing to do with it. They sent me an application, and I had to go to a doctor, take a physical, and do all kinds of things to be sure I was physically able to handle a guide dog.

I was accepted and went to Nashville to get on a plane. I'd never ridden on a jet before. The takeoff was great, but boy, when you can't see, that landing is a doozie. I thought, *Man, is this dude going to stop, or is he going to run over something?* He had the wings tilted or the tail stuck up in the air, or whatever it was. I don't know what it was, but he was coming in fast and slowing down very slow. Well it stopped, and I got off in Newark, New Jersey. Someone from Seeing Eye met me at the airport.

When I arrived in Morristown to receive my first dog, it was a very exciting time. There was a lot of apprehension—What am I going to do? How are this dog and I going to cooperate? Will he or she do what I want it to do? To begin with, you don't know whether you're going to get a male or female, but I asked for a female shepherd.

Out to the school we went. We went through an orientation program, and they gave us a room. I had a roommate who was, by far, above my abilities. He was an appellate court judge for the state of Illinois, of which there are only three. There was no smoking in the rooms, but you can betcha this appellate court judge smoked a cigar in the room, and I don't think anybody ever told him to put it out.

I was using a cane then, but it wasn't long before the trainers took it. They said, "You put that thing up. You don't be using that no more."

I protested, "I use that to keep from running over things!"

They replied, "Well if you run over something, you just run over something."

I walked with the instructor, holding onto the harness the dog wears, and he checked to see how I walk, what my stride is, and what my strength is. Then we meet, and they decide which dog is the one I need.

That first night they brought in a dog. I thought, *Oh, man, what is this?* I got a female shepherd. Her name was Twiggy, but she did not fit her name. This dog weighed sixty-seven pounds, and she was nineteen months old. When you get the dog, it goes everywhere with you on a leash. If you go to the potty room, the dog goes, too. When you go to bed, you hook the dog beside the bed. You've got to get used to her, and everywhere you go, you have the dog on a leash.

The first day I went out at Seeing Eye with her in the harness I was thrilled but still scared. It's hard to tell how you feel. It's more like your freedom than anything else; you can step out and walk and not be afraid.

Seeing Eye in Morristown, New Jersey, is open to the public, and you can go by and see what a great institution and organization it is. Everything is set up just like it would be for a sighted person. The only thing in the whole building that is different is there are cutouts in the rugs that indicate where certain things may be—maybe to the front door, maybe to wherever you want to go. If you miss a cutout, you back up and start over again.

The biggest problem with most blind people is they are scared—scared of the unknown. How do you know what's out there? Do you know where the curb is? Do you think those cars will stop? Do you think you'll run into something or hit someone with the cane? There's always something, and the next thing you know, you're staying home and not going anywhere.

We walked probably a mile or maybe a mile and half, and we came to curbs and corners, and they'd show you what to do. The instructor is right beside you almost all the time. You always do this, do that, and the dog had been trained or educated for three months before we got there. But in reality, she has just been roughly trained. You have to sort of smooth it out and get it to do what you want the dog to.

When you are walking down the street, the dog is dodging this, dodging that, but you don't know what it is dodging. But you better dodge, too, because the dog might say, "I'm going around a tree or around a post." And if you don't go around, you sort of kiss that post or tree. Maybe at the next corner we need to turn right, turn left, or cross the street. Well the instructor is there, and you step out into the street. You hear these cars and say, "Oh man, is that car going to stop?" And you get across the street and are so tickled you just give the dog a big pat, because how many times have you crossed a street and wondered if you would make it? Well that's what the dog does. It protects you against automobiles. The dog's main purpose is to be sure you survive and get home safely.

Each morning for three or four days we took this trip. Then the instructor said, "Well boys and girls, you are going to have to do it on your on today." I thought, *Aw, man I don't know where to go.* But off we went. We'd get to the corner, and I'd say, "I think I turn left here." So I stopped and told the dog to go left, and away we went. Of course we made mistakes, and the instructors corrected us and told us what we needed to do. That afternoon we'd do the same thing again.

Before the week was out, we had started on another walk, which was probably about two and one-half to three miles. There were all kinds of obstacles. Anything you would run into at home was on this path, including overhangs, which the dog had to watch for. I've heard many times, "Well, a dog can't think." That's wrong. The dog has got to think. When it looks up and sees a branch hangs down, its thinking, *Can I go under there without this guy hitting it, because if I hit it, what he is going to do.* So the dog will veer around the branch and go another way.

They have various obstacles are set up at different places. One is where you go into a big box-like structure. When you go in, you're lost; you don't know where to go. So you just keep giving the dog a direction to go until finally it finds the way out.

In another the dog goes to the curb and stops, hopefully, and then out and around the obstacles. If the dog comes to an obstacle blocking your path, you give it directions to where you want to go. Like go to the edge of the street. You go to the edge of the street, it stops, and you step out into the street if nothing is coming—always letting the dog go first. The dog will go as long as you give it directions. You cross the street and continue on your merry way. Your first time at Seeing Eye this process takes four weeks.

They have what is known as the schoolhouse walk. That dude is a tough cookie! I don't know how long it is—probably four miles or more—and you had to do that twice a day. At the end of this, you got to do it on your own. That's not an easy process. You go up the street, cross it, and in the middle of nowhere is a little island. That's all it is, just a little island. You get up on it, and it's got umpteen hundred cars going back and forth like racehorses. When the light changes, you go, and hopefully, you find the little step up in the middle. Then you go across it, stop, and go down across the street again. Then you head up to the school. You go past the school with children and everything else out there, and the dog has got to do what it is supposed to do. Miss all the children, not stop, don't be petted, there's a dog out there—don't pay attention to the dog. You go to the next corner or wherever you're going and decide whether you're crossing the street. Occasionally you make mistakes.

One time I was going down the street, and this lady was with me. and I asked, "Do you know which way to go?"

She said, "No."

"Well, I don't either."

"What are we going to do?"

"We'll walk until we get stopped. The trainer is right behind us, and when he gets tired of walking, he'll stop, turn us around, and head us in the right direction."

Well we crossed the street, and this guy said something to us about going the wrong way or something. I didn't know what he was saying, so I just kept trucking. It wasn't long before the trainer said, "I'm getting a little tired! We're going out in the country. If you're going back to the school, we're going to have to try and go back." So we knew that things were going to be all right.

Anyone heading up into New Jersey, especially around Morristown, should stop in at Seeing Eye and see what a great job these people do with training these dogs to get us out on the street. When you are up there training, you walk a lot. You can walk your shoes down to the soles. Usually you go out in the morning and walk two or three miles, whatever the case may be. It's the same in the afternoon. Sometimes you're walking three or four miles in the morning and three or four miles in the afternoon. It gets to be a very tough trip.

When you go to receive your first guide dog, you stay at the school for four weeks. You are taught many things. You and the dog bond and, hopefully, you will be a great working pair. When you have to get a replacement dog, you stay three weeks. Usually by the end of the second week, everybody's about ready to go home with their replacement. We've been down that road too many times.

CHAPTER 12

GUIDE DOG TRAINERS

The first trainer was Fred Kreitzer. He slipped out of Czechoslovakia (or was it Hungary? I'm not real sure on this) and came to the United States. He was from the old country, and he passed on some of his ways. He was stern; he believed in discipline and obedience. He was a much-disciplined guy and a very good guy. Everything had to be exactly right for him, and the dog had to work exactly the way Fred wanted it to. He had learned the hard way. He started in the dog kennels at Seeing Eye, cleaning out the kennels and worked up to being an instructor. Fred trained Twiggy.

The second guy that I had as an instructor was Pete Lang. Pete was from Ohio and an excellent trainer. As a matter of fact, he sort of guided a lot of the others as to what they should do. Pete worked his way from instructor to become head of all the instructors, which is a pretty influential role when you are at Seeing Eye.

My next instructor was a woman, Leigh Johnson. She trained my third dog, which was Gina. Gina liked the trainer so well, it didn't want to leave her when we were out working. The dog would keep turning around and say, *Where is my instructor? I need to keep up with her, because she's a really good person.* Leigh was not like a lot of the other instructors I had. She was very quiet, subtle, and paid a lot of attention to the dog, which the dog liked, but it made it tougher for the dog to break its bond with her and go with me.

The next instructor I had was named Will Henry. He was from Abingdon, Virginia, and was a very likable guy. He was full of fun and really liked to get out and have a good time with the dogs, making them work and do what they should do. He worked us pretty hard.

People think when you are working with a guide dog, *Well that's easy! The dog just does its thing.* What people don't know is that dog is dodging people, manholes, whatever else is out there, and it does some quick turns to the left and right. And the dog will stop real quick, so you have to be prepared for each movement it makes. The dog's harness is your way of identifying what the dog is going to do. You can feel all of its movements in the harness, so you'd better be prepared.

Will made a point to come to my house on several occasions. My wife cooked some really great fried chicken, and Will was a great eater. He could eat a whole chicken before you could say, "Scat!"

My last trainer was Rivi Israel. She was fairly new to training, and sometimes she didn't think things were going the way she thought they should. In reality, the dog and I were doing what we should have been doing.

I remember one time the dog I currently have, Kenny—or Ken as he's supposed to be called—ran over a curb. Well I corrected him rather hard, and she didn't think I should have done that. She didn't realize that if the dog runs over the curb, the first thing out in the street is you. She didn't think you should be very harsh to the dog, but if you're out on the street and it makes a mistake and let them get away with it, it would be like not disciplining your children. If you give the dogs an inch by not disciplining them properly, they'll take a mile.

We had this one instructor up there—I don't know his name—but he was from Spain. When he brought the dog to the corner, he would say, "Shit!" And everybody around would look to see what in the world he meant. They said this trainer would look around and just grin, and he thought he'd really done well. What he was really saying was, "Sit!" but the way it came out, didn't sound exactly like that.

Georgia Mai and Mike

Martha Lorance Shipp and Georgia Mai   *Mike and Laddie*

Mike before he went blind   *Hershel Lorance*

Trish when Mike could see

Trish now

Mike and his dad

It's a keeper!

Tying a hook and sinker

A happy fisherman

CHAPTER 13

PARTNERS

B ack in Murfreesboro, I was walking around the square one day with Twiggy, and I came to the corner. A gentleman came up beside me and he asked, "Is this a dog guide?"

I said, "Yes, sir, it is."

He asked, "Who are you training it for?"

I said, "I'm not training it for anybody. I'm using it." When this individual passed away, he left some money to Seeing Eye, so I guess I was a good representative.

To show you how advanced people were about dog guides when I got my first one in 1968, I went to the courthouse to collect on a bad check. I had to take out a warrant. While I was standing there waiting, this guy came up and looked down at my dog and the harness. He asked, "What in the world is that on the dog's back?"

"That's my harness, and that's how I plow my garden." He never knew any different.

One time I was asked to go to several schools to speak and take my guide dog. I did. You name it, and I was there. I was asked to go to Shelbyville, Nashville, and Lebanon. I went to Middle Tennessee State, and I got a return call, so I had to go out there again.

I was also requested to take my dog and to grammar schools in Rutherford County. I went to some of the third and fourth grades. I would have all the classes come together, and I would show a film on how the dogs were trained and what to do when you meet one. This seemed to be quite a success for the children, but they were not really interested in the film. They wanted to see what the dog could do.

I'm sure years of appearing before these children and telling them what to do and how to treat the dogs have gone a long way in teaching people how to be aware of and treat guide dogs when they are working. I would talk to these children about blindness and guide dogs. Then I would ask them if they had any questions. You cannot believe some of the questions they would ask. Children are very straightforward; they don't beat around the bush. This one youngster asked me, "Do you dream in color?" I never thought of it like that, but as I had once been able to see, I did dream in color. As I met new people, I would hear their voice, but in my mind, I could not picture a face. I would not know what color hair or eyes were or a lot of other things about them. In my dreams, I would just hear their voice and see their body but not their face.

Guide dogs have always been an important part of my life after I went blind. They were my mode of travel, my friends, my buddies, and my protectors. People don't realize the many things they do. I wasn't going to stay home; I had too much I wanted to do. That was where Twiggy came in. I would hook up the harness and have Ruby drop me off a mile or two from where I was working at Friedman's, and Twiggy and I would walk to work.

One time this woman came up to Ruby at State Farm and said, "You're the cruelest woman I have ever seen!" and Ruby wanted to know why. "Well, you put your husband out on the corner and just let him go,"

Ruby explained, "He gets out on the corner because he wants to go, not because I want him to."

Twiggy and I became a mainstay around the town. We went everywhere we were allowed to enter and accomplished a lot. I thought if I did what I was supposed to do, sooner or later, people in the town would accept a guide dog. Eventually, they did come around to that way of thinking.

Each dog has particular traits. You just have to figure out what they are. Twiggy, for instance, didn't want anybody on her left side. If you walked on her left side, she would do one of two things: she either cut you off or ran you out into the street. If we came to a corner and somebody was standing on her left side, she'd take that big ol' head and move them out of the way. She weighed ninety-eight pounds, so I didn't have a lot of problems.

It's always a tragedy when you have to put down your guide dog. It's really a great loss. Then you have to go get another one and start anew. I'm on my fifth guide dog, so I have done this many times. And it never gets easier.

People are always watching us. They want to know, "Well, did the dog do this? Did the dog do that?" They are always looking for mistakes, not looking to see how well the dog has done and how many times I have crossed the street and not gotten hit by a car. Or how I have gone through crowds of people and not run over anyone. Or how we can go through a doorway; the dogs stick their nose up to the doorknob, where you can find it. Not many people know that. Those are the types of things people tend to ignore.

These dogs have one thing in mind: watch out for the master and take care of him or her. Having your hand on someone's shoulder and following them can work well, except they may forget that when they step off the curb, it's a long way down when you don't know it's coming. A guide dog doesn't do that very often. They will overrun a curb occasionally, but they usually just stop dead still when they hit the edge of the street.

I was asked to attend many places in Murfreesboro and the surrounding areas. I was invited to go places to show my dog, tell them what it is, and the things that I have done. In Shelbyville, Tennessee, I went to the Lions Club. That was an experience, because they didn't really know a lot about guide dogs. It was exciting to me, because I told someone, "I have had guide dogs for so many years, I think I'm an expert."

People ask me, "Do you take your dog with you when you go fishing?" Well I rarely do. The dog would get hair in the boat, and when you get hair in the carpet in the boat, you can hardly get it out—even with a vacuum cleaner.

As I've said before, I got my first guide dog in 1968. Her name was Twiggy. She was exceptional and became one of the family in a hurry. She was what is known as a straight-line dog. She'd start at one corner and go straight to the next corner. She was a big dog; after she gained her full height and build, she weighed about ninety-eight pounds. By the way, she pulled like a mule, too.

I learned a lot from Twiggy, and I hope she learned a little from me. There are many guide dog schools in the country now, but in my opinion, Seeing Eye is the best. In those days, when you went for your first dog, you were at school for four weeks. During this time there was a training program for you and your dog. You got used to the dog and the dog became accustomed to you and what you wanted. In Seeing Eye, they say they don't train the dog—they educate the dog. And after you use the dog for a while, you find out it is pretty well educated.

Twiggy was a lady. She never growled at anyone, and she never barked. And because of her, I never got hit by a car, either. She would go fishing with us on occasion, and she thought that the front seat belonged to her. She would wrap around this pedestal on the front seat, and no matter what you did, she was not about to move. All the guys I fished with knew that was Twiggy's place. You didn't need to bother her, because she was not going to bother you. And she was definitely not going to move. She was going to stay there regardless, and she was too big to argue with.

Guide dogs are not taught to be protective. But they are, because they think you belong to them instead of them belonging to you. Ruby, our daughter, Trish, and I went to Florida one year. Ruby and her sisters went to Disney World and left me by myself. I decided I would go to Daytona and have dinner that night. Well I had dinner and when I came back, I had to take out my dogs. I had a little toy poodle about two or three pounds and this big shepherd.

We went out between the two streets for them to do their nightly chore, and the wind was blowing. While I was standing there with my back to the wind, the little poodle was visible, but the big dog was not. I had her on a long leash, and she was back under a bush. All of a sudden, she came out from under that bush, snarling, which was very unusual. There was a guy standing right behind me, apparently getting ready to do me bodily harm. But when she came out from under that bush, he took off, running and yelling, "Please don't turn the dog loose!" So I had to give Twiggy a little extra petting that night.

I kept Twiggy until August of 1978—that's ten years with one dog. She lived to be about twelve years old and then I had to put her down because of her health problems.

I went back to Seeing Eye and got a guide dog named Biddy. Well she fit her name perfectly. She was like a biddy—she was into everything! I don't care what you did, she would always mess up. But the one thing she did is make sure I got across the street in one piece. Sometimes I thought that was a miracle!

We were going to Lake Eufaula fishing one time, and she was hooked in the back of my station wagon. We went to dinner, and when we got back, I looked for my big bag of Oreo cookies—one that had three rows in it. Guess what? Biddy had eaten every one of those cookies!

Biddy liked to show off in front of people. She'd just parade, dance, and do her stuff. But she was very good when it came to taking care of me. The trainer for Biddy was Pete Lang, who later became one of the top trainers for Seeing Eye.

The next guide dog I received was named Gina. She was something else. She was very smart, very loyal, and did everything she was supposed to do. She was quiet and didn't cause any trouble, but there was one thing. She did not like other dogs for some reason.

Gina was very protective and very obedient and just a super nice dog. She took care of me in lots and lots of ways, and I managed to take care of my business for many years with her help. My trainer for Gina was Leigh Johnson, and she did a good job. For many years, Gina was always exactly what I needed, and I wanted to thank her every chance I got.

In 2000 I went to get Roxie. Roxie was different. She was very loyal, wanted to play a lot, and was very attentive to everyone. She was outstanding when it came to working on the street. She did her job better than most. Her trainer was Will Henry.

In 2007 I received the dog I have now. When I went to Seeing Eye to get my new dog, which turned out to be Ken, they asked me what I wanted. I said, "I want another female shepherd." The reason I wanted a female is because if I went fishing in the daytime, the females would take care of themselves, and I wouldn't have to worry about them until I came in late that afternoon. Males might have been a little different.

They kept asking me, "Would you like to have a male? Would you take a male?" I kept saying no, but I finally agreed. Well guess what? Before I could say, "Scat!" there was Ken. Ken is a big, long-hair, male shepherd. When I say long hair, that's a throwback to many hundreds of years ago, when I guess all the German shepherds had really long hair to protect them when they were fighting off wolves and coyotes.

When I received him, he was like me; he was tall but a little on the skinny side. With all the work we go through when we go to the school to pick up the dog, I can understand why they are skinny, and I didn't gain any weight either. His long hair continued to grow, and one of the trainers said, "Oh, it won't be any trouble. It won't be much hair."

They didn't know what they were talking about. With that dog, it's hard to keep your rug clean. His hair got so long, I started having him trimmed about every six weeks, because he was like a sweeper. His hair would pick up dirt, leaves, and everything else and bring it into the house.

Ken was different. I had not had a male guide dog, and they are a little different from the females. One thing different is they always want to stick their nose where it doesn't need to be. But he finally came around to my way of seeing things and is an excellent guide dog. Leigh Johnson had a big hand in his training also.

I've had Kenny for several years now, and he is outstanding. He has saved my goose on more than one occasion. When you live in Murfreesboro, where the traffic is "everybody for themselves," you'd better be prepared for anything. I know I've started across the street and cars got awfully close, so when Ken puts on the brakes, I put on the brakes. Kenny is one thing that makes me the way I am, I suppose. He gives me the freedom to go and do the things I want to do, and people can't say, "Well the poor, old, blind guy, he can't do nothing!"

People continually ask me, "Is your dog full blooded?"

I tell them, "I can run his pedigree back farther than I can run my own." Everywhere I go with Kenny, someone is always talking about what a beautiful dog he is. I'm sure he is, but having only been able to feel his long hair and how he acts, I guess I don't really know how pretty he is. I just think I do. When I speak to a group of people, if I can, I take my guide dog. Kenny's like my right-hand man. He does everything I expect him to do and takes care of me. I've had five guide dogs and multiple trainers, and each trainer is a little different than the others.

When you're walking down the street, these dogs walk between three and four miles an hour. There is a reason for this. Number one is if you're walking fast, people can't sit there and watch you as you go down the street, but they still watch as far as they can. When I first started using a guide dog in Murfreesboro, I was a little self-conscious about people watching me. But after a while, I got used to it. Even though I have done this for many years, I can walk down the street and still tell when somebody's watching to see what we are doing. Guide dogs have played a great part in my life as far as fishing or anything else goes. They've kept me independent and mobile, and for that reason, I'm able to fish and do the things I do.

Over the years I've had a guide dog, they have been a great inspiration to me in my travels. They opened many doors, and I've met many, people because of these dogs. They give a blind person confidence. You can go where you want to go. If somebody doesn't feel like taking you, call a cab and go. If you want to go to Nashville or wherever else you might want to go, the dog is always ready to go and will work rain, snow, sleet, or shine. You may not want to go, but the guide dog is always willing.

Chapter 14

Coping with Blindness

When I returned to Murfreesboro with my first guide dog, things didn't get any easier. When you go to town there was always do this, do that, gotta go here, and gotta go there, going to stores is always the same. The dog knew what to do when you got in the stores, but the people in Murfreesboro didn't know what to do.

I'd go into a store and they'd say, "You can't bring that dog in here. You've got to go."

I'd say, "It's a guide dog, and state law says we can go into public buildings."

They'd answer, "You can't come in here!"

"Okay."

I'd had so much trouble with businesses and people in Murfreesboro that I went to see attorney Guy Dotson. Guy later became the county district attorney. Guy and I sat down, and he said, "I tell you what you do. The next time someone gives you a problem with this, you come and see me, and we'll go take care of that problem." I thought, *Well, that might be a good idea.* But when I left, I got to thinking, *You know, if I cause a lot of trouble, a lot of people will not want me to come in whether they say anything or not.* So the next time it happened, I decided I'd just take my medicine and go on my merry way. But after a while, people began to let us go into their businesses without any problems.

I had other problems, too. People didn't realize I was blind. I was able to look someone in the eye and follow his or her voice. I guess that goes back to when I was able to see. People didn't realize I was blind, and often when I told them, they would be flabbergasted. They didn't realize how much time and effort were put into letting people know I am more than just a blind person.

This world is for sighted people, not blind people. I hear people say all the time, "Aw, he's not handicapped. He can still get around." But when you are blind, you have to have help in everything you do. If you're going to town, you've got to have someone else to get you there. You may have a guide dog, but that dog can only do so much. There's no need to go to a movie, because you can't see the pictures. You can hear it, but you can stay at home and do the same thing. You go to a restaurant. Most menus are not in Braille. Being handicapped causes a world of problems, and nobody knows how many problems until they are in that particular situation.

If you can see and you make a wrong turn, you can read street signs or recognize buildings to get going in the right direction. If you're blind and you get lost you have to ask somebody. If there's no one to ask you wander around until you find your way and that can take hours. It seemed everything I wanted to do I had to rely on someone else.

Then I made a decision that I guess changed my life. It had to be for the better, because it certainly couldn't have gotten any worse. I joined the church. I've heard people say many times, "Take it to the Lord, and He'll take care of you." That's exactly what I did, and He did exactly that. Things started to smooth out, and I guess my life became a whole lot better, and probably my wife's and daughter's lives as well. When you're blind, you get frustrated easily, and whatever it is, you've got to take it out on somebody. Many times I'm sure it was my wife or my daughter, and for that, I am very sorry.

I could tell daylight from dark, but it became so hard to do that I really didn't pay any attention to it. If it was dark, it didn't bother me; if it was light, it didn't bother me. People would ask me, "What can you see?" Well, I couldn't see anything.

When I first went blind and lost my job, times were really tough. One time we needed coal for our furnace. A half a ton of coal was six dollars. Guess what? I didn't even have six dollars to buy the coal. I didn't even know where our next meal was coming from because I didn't have a job and I didn't know how to find one. I now know what people mean when they say they were desperate. I was desperate. I didn't know what I was going to do, but like I said, that was when I turned to the church. I joined the church, and life became a whole lot better.

During this time, I made a point of learning to pick up voices when dealing with people. When I found someone's voice, I'd have a good idea where he or she was, and that way, I could follow his or her movements. Sometimes people said things that didn't mean anything except to me. That way, when someone spoke, not only would I know where the person was, I'd often know what he or she was thinking.

This gave me a little confidence in speaking to and in front of people. I began to give myself a little freedom by going out more and mixing with other people. It didn't take long before I received a call from a woman in Smyrna, Tennessee. She said, "I've got a 105 Cub Scouts coming. Could you come and speak to these kids?"

I said, "I'll be glad to," and down I went. What a group—105 kids! I guess they were about seven or eight years old, but I'm not sure. I split them into two groups, half in the morning and half in the afternoon. The first half of the morning, I talked to them about fishing and the other half of that morning, I talked to them about blindness. That afternoon I switched it around— first half on blindness and other half on fishing. Then, I started asking questions: "What would you like to know? Have you got any questions on fishing?" Well, they did, and I answered all of them.

Then I asked, "Do you have any questions on blindness?" Well, there were a lot of questions on blindness, and I answered them, too.

I spoke to Cub Scout groups for several years, until the provider of my transportation, Ruby, passed away. I was no longer able to get back and forth to Smyrna.

A lot of blind people are afraid of the unknown. They are afraid to go out into the world; they are afraid to go anywhere when they don't know what will happen. Well you've just got to buckle up and get it done. Everything you try to do as a blind person requires more effort.

Suppose you drop a screw or whatever on the floor. You might have to get down there and hunt for it. That takes extra effort, and a lot of people won't do that either. Whenever you have a chore—vacuum your house, wash your clothes, wash your boat, or whatever—you have to find a way to do it, because it's likely nobody else is going to do it for you. Before my wife passed away, I did have help in a lot of things that I wanted to do, but after she died, everything was sort of do it myself or it doesn't get done.

I have been asked to do many things because I am blind. I was asked to talk with people who were going blind; some of them were already blind. They all had the same problem; they all had self-pity. When they asked me what they should do, I would tell them, "First look around or check around. You'll find there are a lot of people out there who are pulling for you. If you'll also stop and think, you'll realize you're not treating your family very well when you sit over in the corner or become belligerent or have a lot of self-pity. There are still a lot of things you can do. All you have to do is apply yourself and work a little harder than maybe the next guy."

I was invited out to a class at the university, and there are some things that people always ask me: "What color hair do I have? What color of eyes do I have? About how tall am I?" Over the years, I have learned a few things. One thing is to always underestimate weight. You always overestimate what they look like in a positive manner. I became quite proficient at guessing what color of hair someone might have, what color eyes one might have, and maybe something else, but I always exaggerated other things.

Many years ago, I started writing an outdoor column for the *Daily News Journal* in Murfreesboro, and it is published weekly. I guess it is one of the longer published articles in our area. They ran a survey one time to see what article is read first in the *News Journal,* and they picked my outdoor column as the first thing they read, but I didn't get any plaques for it. Many if not most of the people who read my column do not know I am blind. If they did, they probably wouldn't read it. They'd think I didn't know what I was doing.

A lot of opportunities were presented to me as a blind person. I was probably a little on the unique side. I don't know whether that was good or bad, but I had opportunities to go fishing in many areas in and out of the state of Tennessee. There were few times that anyone ever said anything about me being blind, at least that I heard. I caused no problems; I became no handicap to my fishing partners, so I was accepted in all of the fishing groups.

I also became the first blind person in Rutherford County to be admitted into the Masonic Lodge. It took a little doing, but that was managed, and I've been a member of the lodge for over forty years. I was willing to do anything to help me become a better person and be able to handle my disability as best I could.

As I grew older, I made it a point to make sure children knew there was a difference in being blind and handicapped. Being handicapped can mean you really don't want to do anything and not doing anything in a lot of cases. When I had my guide dog, I would explain to the children what it did. I explained there are some things blind people cannot do, such as drive a car or a fishing boat. You are dependant on people to do these things for you, but there is a lot you can do.

I also spoke to third-graders at some area schools and showed a film about guide dogs. I visited many schools in the middle Tennessee area and was warmly received, especially by the children, because I had a big dog with me. I was also a guest at Middle Tennessee State University for a couple of guys. They all got A's. What did I get? A ride home!

I fished a lot of the area lakes before I went blind, and I probably waded every river in the area that you can think of. I still remember exactly how everything was. The conclusion is that growing old has one meaning—you're building memories.

I have had the opportunity to fish more lakes than you can believe. Being blind, this is something that is hard to believe and hard to imagine, but it sure has been great! Each year, the local Lions Club has a fishing tournament. It's called the Tournament for Sight. I do my best to find sponsors to contribute to this event. I have been told that I have raised more money for the Lions Club than anyone else. This always makes me feel good, because it goes for a great cause. When I go to talk to someone, he or she believes me because I am blind and know what it is like. I can pass along the information that will maybe make them want to contribute a bit more.

I've had the privilege of being the first blind person in these tournaments, but I always pay my own entry fee. They say, "Aw, you shouldn't pay!" But I think I should, and I always do. The best I've done in these tournaments is second. That's pretty good, considering there are usually 75 to 125 folks in these tournaments. There have been very few times that I didn't go home with some of the prize money.

I was in a big restaurant one time, and the manager came up to me when I was seated and he said, "I've been the manager of this restaurant for ten years—it's a big restaurant, also—and you are the first person to be in this restaurant with a guide dog." I thought that was unusual, but it also speaks to what kind of problems blind people must face.

Being blind is always makes it a challenge to accomplish what you want to do. You've got to figure out a way. One day I was out in my garage, getting some fishing tackle ready for a tournament that night, and a bee just kept flying and flying around me. I thought, *You sorry thing! I'll get rid of you!* So I lowered the door to the garage. Well my garage has no windows. I always tell everybody, "I can't see out, and doesn't anybody need to see in." Well the bee kept flying, and it was dark in there. It hit the boat and got inside the boat. I got in there with a badminton racket and was whacking at him. Boy, I was wearing him out. My wife came out the back, hollering, "What's going on?" I finally got the bee cornered in the bottom of the boat, and I whacked him until I killed him. Then I raised the garage door and told my wife I was killing a bee. Of course, that brought a lot of talk from her also.

Being blind, you try to accomplish something to keep people from thinking you are not a sighted, though they know differently. My problem was either I was doing too good a job or people didn't care. I have been left everywhere! We were fishing a tournament on Smith Lake one time and stopped to get some gas. We were all standing out there, and all of a sudden, everybody disappeared. I was standing in the middle of the parking lot with no idea of where to go. Somebody finally came back to get me.

Having a guide dog has really enriched my life. It has made me try even harder to accomplish whatever it is I want to do. My guide dog has given me mobility and, of course, a lot of attention from people who admire my dog. One morning I went into the bank. They let me in a little early, because they knew I wasn't going to rob the bank since I couldn't see where the guard was. I spoke to a teller I knew, and while I was there, they were giving a group of children a tour of the bank and showing them how it operated.

What they were showing the children about the bank went by the wayside when they saw the dog. The teacher was from Lascassas, and her name was Mrs. Florida. I told her, "If these children are interested in the dog, I'd be glad to tell them all I can about the dog." So they gathered around. I started explaining to these children what the dog did, what role he played in my life, and how they were supposed to treat him. I then explained to the children some of the things the dog did, like how he prevented me from getting run over in traffic, how he found doors for me, and how he helped me avoid people obstacles. I told them anything that might have been of interest to the children.

The next time I went into the bank, some of the employees came up to me and said, "You know, we learned more about guide dogs when you were talking to those children than we ever dreamed we could." I thought that was a great compliment.

Two of the more important things in my life were guide dogs, which gave me mobility and the opportunity to do some of the things I managed to do, and the other would have to be fishing. It was a love that I still have today. At one time, I really liked to hunt, but when you lose your sight, hunting is sort of out of the question, especially since no one wants to go with you.

I'd been doing television shows on different things, and one time I thought, *I believe I can shoot a pheasant.* So I called this pheasant farm in Springfield, Tennessee, and I told him, "I would like to come up and hunt pheasants."

He said, "That's great! Come ahead!"

"There's only one small problem."

"What's that?"

"I'm blind."

There was a long pause. Then he said, "Well, we're open for business."

I had thought when a pheasant comes up, it makes an awful lot of racket, and I believed I could follow him and hit him with some cylinder bore shotgun. But I never got that opportunity. I decided to do something else instead of the pheasant show. I have been invited to go duck hunting several times, but I wonder who would be in more danger—the duck hunters or the ducks?

I've been invited to Middle Tennessee State University several times to speak to their fishing class. There are a lot of people they could invite, but they came up with a blind guy who's going to show all these folks how to fish. There's one thing I always try to show these beginning fishermen: how to get a hook out of your hand. Getting a hook in your hand seems to happen to a lot of people. If you are around hooks, there is one of them that is going to get you.

I usually ask for a volunteer, and when I tell them what I want a volunteer for, the volunteers disappear. So I'll stick a fishhook in the corner of my finger. It doesn't hurt. When I stick the hook in my hand, you can hear aahs and eehs all over the place. That gets them excited and grabs their attention. Then I show them how to get it out.

I have managed to get fishhooks out of a lot of people with this particular method. To remove the hook, take some strong fishing line and loop it around the hook, take your finger and bend the eye of the hook. Then give it a quick little pop, and guess what? Out will fly the hook, and it won't hurt a bit. I've been thinking I might start charging surgeon's fees to remove these hooks.

People ask me how I fish. I tell them with a lot of hard work. There is one thing I have that seems to be a problem with most blind people: equilibrium. When you're standing in a boat, it is rocking and rolling, and waves going in and out from under the boat keep you vibrating back and forth. If your equilibrium is off, the next thing you know is you'll be in the lake. I don't know why mine is good, but it is. I can stand up with big waves hitting the boat, bouncing it around, and it never seems to bother me. I can feel the waves coming under the bottom of the boat, and from experience, I know which way to go. I have been in waves up to eight feet high in a bass boat, and that's pretty tough.

With patience, diligence and hard work you can figure out a way to do most anything even if you are blind. It's not easy and it takes a lot of time but you can eventually figure out a way to do the job. You can put something up and say, "By jingoes, I know exactly where it's at." Well guess what? When you get there, it's not there. *Well what did I do with it?* Not being able to see, you've just got to guess. You start looking and feeling and eventually you'll run across it somewhere.

I did, however, put away the titles to two vehicles I own. I said, "I know exactly where they are." I've not found those titles, so I really did a good job of hiding them.

CHAPTER 15

OPPORTUNITIES

I guess as you get older, you reminisce about what happened years ago and you wonder what's going to happen in the future. I had the store down at Jackson Heights shopping center for about six or seven years and then decided I needed to do something else. I was stuck down there, and it was taking all my time. I was not really getting to enjoy life. I remembered I enjoyed fishing too much and I wanted to do more fishing in the future.

So I went to work at Friedman's, which was on the corner of Walnut and West Main Street. The owner of the store was John Friedman, and he and I got along fine. I took over the back of the store and ran the sporting goods department—firearms, fishing, camping, archery—all these things. When you run a store like I was, you learn a lot about guns quickly and what to look for and where you think something may be wrong with it. I applied that same principle at Friedman's. I did a lot of gun trading and a lot of buying of firearms at Friedman's and made some really good deals. I bought some really nice guns and made John pretty happy, I suppose.

When I went to work at Friedman's after I closed Mike's Sport Shop, everybody I ran into seemed to think I was putting on—that I could see. The first thing they would ask me was, "Well, how much can you see?" They didn't really want to believe I couldn't see anything. Hunters would come in and figure they were going to hoodoo me when they tried to trade guns. Well that's a bad way to think about things, because I knew a lot more about guns than they did.

We sold a lot of guns at Friedman's; as a matter of fact, I probably sold more than my share. I had this young woman come in one time and want to buy a pistol. I sold her a pistol, but it had to be approved through the sheriff's department, and we couldn't get it done on a Friday afternoon. I told her we'd have to turn the papers in, and she could come on Monday or Tuesday and pick up the pistol if everything was okay. She filled out the forms the way they were supposed to be, including the pistol permit and a 4473 license form, a required federal form to purchase firearms.

When we received the pistol permit back from the sheriff's office, he had one question marked. On that application the question was, "Have you ever been committed to a mental institution?" She had answered no. Then she added, "Well, I had amnesia one time." At the very end, she signed it, but at that time, the sheriff could not go and check on medical records. But he signed the permit for her to have a pistol. She came in on Monday morning to pick up her firearm and left. The following weekend, we learned she had gone back to her home in Atlanta and shot herself with that pistol. Then all heck broke loose.

Her parents filed a big lawsuit against Friedman's for selling her a firearm though she had been committed to a mental institution; we did not know that at the time. Well it was a long, drawn-out case, and in the end, we all had to go to court. Everybody was questioned, and they had me in the very back room, away from everybody else. I was going to be the last witness. They went through all the witnesses and then they came to get me. I thought they had forgotten me. When I got on the witness stand, it didn't take long to figure out that these people didn't know much about firearms and very little about the laws and regulations.

I said, "Well the only question is was she mentally competent. The only information we have is she signed the form that said she had never been committed to a mental institution, and that should relieve us of all responsibility." The case was thrown out of court.

I was teaching this guy to sell firearms—what he needed to do to show the firearms and whatever was necessary to let the people know they were getting a good firearm. There are always things going on in a gun shop that probably a lot of people don't know. We had sold this particular firearm to a man, and he'd gone out and shot himself. We can't control what they do with the firearms, but the guy's family wanted us to buy it back. Since it had only been fired once, we bought it back. It so happened that my trainee was showing this pistol to someone. He said, "Now this gun is great! It's only been fired once. A guy shot himself with it."

Well you know what happened. Whoever was interested in buying the pistol left town. I told the clerk, "This pistol is in great shape. It doesn't have any blood or anything on it, and you don't need to tell everybody that the guy used it to shoot himself!"

Twiggy was my guide dog when I worked for John. Whenever we had any problems in the store, I'd just take Twiggy to the scene, and we'd break up the problem. One day we had three shoplifters. John caught them. They had made a run for the back door, but it was locked. Twiggy guarded them until the police came with handcuffs and carried them away.

They put me over the guns, the fishing equipment, the archery equipment, and the camping equipment. I met a lot of people there who probably pushed me along my way and did a lot to make me feel good and a little better about myself. I learned a lot more about guns and sold and traded an awful lot of guns. I became very proficient in the handling of firearms. Then there came another challenge. People came in and wanted me to appraise their firearms. Well I proceeded to do that. Sometimes I'd need a little help looking up information, but I got very good at appraising guns. I appraised firearms for insurance companies, homeowners, and individuals. Then came another opportunity.

I was approached to appraise some firearms and work for an attorney, Steve Waldron. We went to court, and I was approved to be an expert witness in divorce cases, as well as anything pertaining to firearms. Anytime he had a divorce case with guns or firearms of any kind in it, he'd call me. Usually he represented the women. Can you imagine a blind guy and his guide dog sitting on the witness stand in the court, with these high-priced attorneys, and telling them what these guns are valued at? It wasn't hard for me to take on these attorneys, because they knew nothing about firearms, and that's what I did know about. We usually won our case without any problems.

I would take the firearms that were listed and research them. Many times I checked out the guns themselves out to make sure exactly what they were. When we got to court, I had everything in my mind that I wanted to do. The attorneys would ask questions, but their questions were minor, because they didn't know what to ask. When I was on the witness stand, it would be me and my guide dog, who would lie on the floor. Even though I was blind, it was obvious I knew what I was doing.

I only worked on behalf of women; the men didn't want me to appraise their firearms, because I had sold them many of the ones they had. While I was going to court appraising firearms, one guy had a little over twenty thousand dollars in firearms. He'd told his wife he didn't have any. Well when I got up in court and went through everything he had, I felt a little bit skittish. He could see, and I couldn't. I was concerned he might decide to run over me or my dog. So working as an appraiser wasn't exactly great all the time. I did receive a lot of appreciation from many of the ladies I helped in their divorce cases, because they got half of everything that I came up with.

When I first went to work for Friedman's in Murfreesboro, John Friedman was the owner. He and his wife, Cheryl, ran the store. John was a good guy to work for. He caused no trouble, and he helped me in every way he could. As a matter of fact, he sponsored some of my fishing tournaments and paid the entry fees. I worked for John for about ten years and then he sold out to a gentleman named Charles Friedman. I sure missed working for John after he sold the store.

Two really nice women worked in the store with me for many years. One was Debbie Fann, and the other one was Delores Galloway. They put in a lot of time and probably didn't make very much money, but both very good when it came to store business.

Even though I've not worked there for many years, I still have people say they'd come in the store and didn't even know I was blind. I guess that's probably due more to Ruby than to me, because she didn't want me to act like I was blind.

I continued fishing and entered just about every tournament I could go to as long as it didn't interfere with my work or taking care of things at home. Word got around. They said, "You know that old blind guy there? He catches a lot of fish!" I started getting invitations from everybody you could think of to go fishing with them. Maybe they thought I knew something they didn't know. People would come into the store and ask me questions about this or whatever, and they would think maybe what I was telling wasn't exactly true. Some people hid in other areas and listened to see if I told the same tale to everybody. Like I told somebody one time, "If you tell the truth the first time, you don't have to worry about what you tell every time after that."

While I was working at Friedman's, another thing came into my life. I was asked to do a weekly column on hunting and fishing for the *Daily News Journal.* So it came—the "Outdoors and Mike" column. I talked about fishing, I talked about hunting, I talked about archery, I talked about camping—whatever came along that pertained to the outdoors was what I used in the column. People asked me how I did all this. I had people at a lot of different lakes that I had known for quite a while, and I would call them, get information, and put it in the column. That way, I could help everybody. I hope a lot of people have enjoyed it. It must have been successful, because I've been there for about twenty-five years.

Dr. Clarence Greever—everybody called him Pete—of Middle Tennessee State University used to come into the store all the time. He read my column. I thought he was an English teacher at the university. I told him, "Dr. Greever, I can't spell cat! I need to go back out to the university and learn to spell."

He said, "No, you don't need to go back out to the university. They'll ruin you!"

I asked, "What do you mean, they'll ruin me?"

He said, "You have a style that when I read your column, it sounds like you're talking to me. And if you go out there they, will do away with all that. So you don't need to go." So guess what? I didn't go.

I had contacts all over middle Tennessee, and whenever I needed information about fishing on a certain lake, I would contact someone I knew on that lake. For instance, Tim Staley on Center Hill Lake.

Tim and I had known each other for several years, and when I became a columnist and needed information, he was always there to provide it for me. Tim would fish a lot of the tournaments on Center Hill and keep me up to date as to where the fish were, how deep they were, and what types of lures were best for people who were having a hard time catching fish.

Percy Priest Lake had a tremendous number of fishermen who were helpful to me. Anytime they caught fish or knew something that would be helpful to other fishermen, they would contact me.

Fate Sanders boat dock was in operation, and Roland Hopkins, better known as Hoppy, was the owner. He went out of his way to do whatever was necessary to provide information about the area fishing. Of course I'm sure it helped his business, also. Hoppy had a son, John Garner Hopkins, and we all went fishing several times. I remember one time we were fishing on Lake Normandy, and John Garner was about twelve years old. I said, "John, you see how close we are to the bank over there? I'm going to throw a lure over there—this artificial worm—and have the tail of it hit the bank." Not having any idea that this could happen, I cast, and guess what? It happened, and I still hear about it from him.

This friend of mine, Randy Bolin, who owns a sport shop in Murfreesboro, Tennessee, was seen taking his pants off and putting them in the car. He had his regular shorts on, which he was going to fish in, but when I got news of that, I put in the paper that Randy Bolin was seen "streaking" across the parking lot at Fate Sanders. Randy went to church the Sunday morning after it came out in the paper, and this little old lady said, "Randy, when are you going to streak again? We'd all like to be there!" Of course I caught a little flak over that, but it was all in fun.

I also did several articles for *Bassmasters* magazine. Fishermen think this is probably one of the best outdoor magazines in the country. I wonder if any of those guys who read my articles realized I was blind.

Over the years, I have many people come up to me and say they purchased an automobile from me. That was a long time ago, also when they didn't know I was blind. Along with trading firearms, pistols, rifles, shotguns, and everything with people in Rutherford County and the surrounding areas, most of those people didn't know I was blind. A gentleman I sold a gun to back in about 1990 came by and said something about purchasing a gun from me. All these things make you feel good. You feel that you have done a halfway decent job to have these people still remember you.

During this time, I met a lot of fishermen—a lot of good fishermen. Some were very famous. As a matter of fact, I met some television stars, and I thought, *You know, that wouldn't be a bad way to make a living."* This motivated me to become a tournament fisherman. There wasn't any blind tournament fisherman out there; leastways I didn't know of any. So I proceeded to study, to do the best I could, and took every opportunity to practice casting. Anything that would help me become a better fisherman was what I did. I went a lot of places and did a lot of things during that period. I don't know why, but it seemed to affect a lot of people, and I got more and more opportunities.

CHAPTER 16

TELEVISION

I had been the instigator in starting the first BASS club in Murfreesboro, known as Murfreesboro Anglers, and quite a few of those guys came in. We had a tournament about once a month at the different area lakes, and during this time, we all learned a lot. Percy Priest Lake had been impounded, and it provided a lot of fishing area for a lot of people, and fishing really started on the upturn.

Then, like the song, *Along Came Jones*, along came the television shows. This was an exciting thing for me to do. I had no idea how to do a TV show—probably still don't—but we started anyway.

Neal Watson, who was a photographer and also great in a lot of other areas with the photography equipment, and I decided we would do a television show. We named it *Outdoors with Mike*. We would cut no slack. We would do whatever it took to get a good show. We fished all the area lakes. We usually had one day to do our show. We didn't have many days to go out and practice, like everybody else did. We all had to work other jobs. This show started on channel thirty-nine, and we had it on twenty cable companies. That was before there was ESPN and all these things they have now.

We couldn't decide what type of opening to have on this TV show. The guys at the TV station came up with this one, and I didn't have anything to do with it. It said, "*Outdoors with Mike,* featuring America's greatest blind fisherman." Well I was asked later, "How do you know you're the greatest blind fisherman?"

I said, "'Cause I don't know any others."

Neal was the cameraman, and he and I made a lot of trips—a lot of fruitless trips but also some real good ones. We filmed on West Point in Georgia. We filmed on Lake Eufaula. We filmed on Center Hill, Tims Ford, Normandy, Percy Priest, and Old Hickory. If there was a place to catch fish, we'd go there. Then we went into the hunting part of the show.

Can you imagine a blind guy in a hunting program? Well the first hunting program we had featured Mike Nunley, Mike Phillips, and Zane Cantrell. We were doing a rabbit show. We got the dogs running, and it was great. We harvested some rabbits and brought those in, and there were a few other little items that happened along the way.

Then I decided, "This is what I think I'll do." We had just filmed somebody shooting a rabbit that was going through the fence. I told them, "I tell you what let's do." I took that shotgun, and as we rolled the film back to where the rabbit went through the fence, I shot, just like I was the one that shot the rabbit. I reached down and picked up the rabbit. When the show aired, the film had been edited showing me shooting, the rabbit doing a flip, and then me picking up the rabbit, saying, "Boys, you can't believe anything you see on television, because I didn't even shoot at the rabbit."

We took people from Murfreesboro and other places to a lot of locations. Some of these shows were good; some probably not so good. We did all kinds of television shows. We did shows where they were chasing wild pigs with dogs. We did dove shows, rabbit shows; if you had something you wanted us to do, we were delighted to do it. We tried to do any kind of outdoor show people would like. We did sauger shows, where we caught a lot of sauger. And boy, they do eat well! We did crappie shows, and we did bass shows.

We'd have the TV show going, and I'd be talking to someone. When you're out there talking, there's only you, the cameraman, and the guy you're talking to. Sometimes it'd be like pulling teeth to get the guest to say anything. You'd think, *This guy right there, he'd talk like a Polly parrot,* but when the camera hit him, he wouldn't say "Mush!"

We did several shows on Center Hill Lake. I had fished Center Hill for many years before I went blind, so I knew a lot of places there to fish. There are always some interesting things happening when you're doing a television show. Some of them you show; some of them you don't.

We had another interesting commercial on the show. I was asked a bunch of times, "Where are you going to drive that Dodge truck this week?" The reason for the question was I did this commercial where I said, "Boy, a Dodge truck will really take off!" My cameraman set up the camera, hit the gas, and spun the wheels. Then I got in there, and it stopped. Then I said, "Man, that thing will stop on a dime!" And I opened the door, and there was a dime right under the wheel, just like I had stopped dead still.

Well when we left, the cameraman was headed back to Murfreesboro; this was shot on Center Hill Lake. He had his wife stand on the side of the bridge with the camera to film him as he drove by. He had on one of my hats, and he waved for the camera as he went by. Everybody thought I was driving that truck.

Arnold Williams, I, and several others were shooting a show about dove hunting. Before we got the camera set up, two doves came across the field. Arnold pulled up his shotgun and downed both of them. We got the cameras all set up and everything working, and here comes another dove. Arnold stood up and shot at him—boom, boom, boom—didn't even raise a feather. When the show aired, the cameraman blew that dove up to about the size of a B-29 so Arnold looked like he couldn't hit the side of a barn.

A big golden retriever worked with us while we shot this episode. Someone shot a dove down, and the retriever brought it back. When the dog opened its mouth for the guy to take the bird, the dove flew off. Apparently someone wasn't a very good shot. They shot a couple more down, and the dog went out but didn't come back. We went to check on him, and we found him with one foot on a bird and another one in his mouth. The dog couldn't figure out how to get the other one in there with it. Well that was some of the things that happened on the dove show that we didn't get to the broadcast.

The more people watch a television program, the more you can charge for advertising, and that's what we were really interested in. We did several shows and did as much as we could in one day, because that's all the time we had. If the weather was bad or something didn't work, we'd have to go in, postpone it, and do it another day.

We did a series of thirteen shows and then we'd have thirteen reruns. That seemed the best way to do it then. We did a lot of television shows on the area lakes, because they were close and could be done in one day. Then we went to other lakes. We went to Lake Eufaula in Alabama and West Point Lake in Georgia and got good shows on both of them.

The first television show we did was on Lake Normandy. It was a tough lake, but we caught a lot of fish. I hooked a fish down in the lower end of the lake on an artificial worm. I was standing in the back of the boat when the fish jumped. Well the fish went one way, and the worm went the other.

The cameraman got a picture of that, and we put it on the start of the television show. I tried to keep my television show local, with people from the local area as guests on the show. I had Don Phillips, who was a Murfreesboro fireman, as a guest and Johnny Mathews, from out at Walter Hill community, as a guest.

Johnny was a great guest! He is now a retired detective from the Murfreesboro Police Department. We were doing a commercial for Coke, and we needed several takes. Every time I'd hand him a Coke, he opened it. When we got through with the takes, he had a whole floor covered with Coke bottles.

We were doing this episode going down this bank, fishing, and Johnny looked up. I'd done caught three or four. He said, "Boy, you are wearing me out!"

I said, "If you'd change lures to like I've got on, you'd probably catch one."

We were upriver, fishing and doing the television show with Lawrence McConnell, who worked at Standard Oil. We had a good show going, and at the end of the show, I caught this big fish. It was a big one—it was probably six or seven pounds—and at that time, it was a nice one. We finished shooting and quit. The next morning, I was setting up at the store, and this gentleman came up and said, "I saw y'all catch that fish down there yesterday afternoon. I'd given twenty dollars to know what you were using."

I said, "If you'd given me twenty dollars I'd given you a handful of what I was using. I was using a Hobo Worm."

I was doing a television show with Don Phillips, who passed away several years back. He was someone I fished with in a lot of tournaments. We were up in a creek, and I caught one. He said, "That's a Hercules man!"

I asked, "What's a Hercules man?"

He said, "He's a giant!" Well, I got the fish in and got it on film. I cast out and hung another one, which I believe was bigger than the other one, and the cameraman ran out of film. In those days, we were using eight-millimeter cameras, and the film only lasted twenty minutes. So we waited around so he could get more film in the camera, and guess what? I lost the fish! It was probably the biggest I ever caught there.

When we were doing these television shows, it was not like it is in modern times. We had our show on twenty cables. Now you put it on one, and it covers the world. Our base station was channel thirty-nine, out of Murfreesboro. This was where all our programs originated. You name it, and we would fish for it. I don't care what it was; we'd go out and try to do a film, especially if it was easy.

In those days, I had a boat sponsor, and I got a new boat about every six months. Somebody asked, "Why are you getting so many boats?"

I replied, "Well, I run it six months and then sell it and buy me another one, hoping to make a little bit." That helped to pay the expenses. Clint Brownlow of Brownlow Manufacturing Company was the one who sponsored me. He was a really nice guy and did a lot to help promote our show.

We had a lot of great sponsors—Coca-Cola, Dodge—you name it we had them on our list at one time or another. Can you imagine these people wanting to sponsor someone who is blind and out hunting or standing up in a fishing boat and walking around while it does all sorts of things? It was great to know they had that much confidence that we would come up with a good show.

We were doing a television show one time with Arnold Williams, Dillard Parsley, and I don't know who all—just a big group of guys from State Farm. Well we had the cooler open and were doing a commercial for Coca-Cola. We were offering everybody Cokes, and when this one particular individual came up out of the field, we asked him if he wanted a Coke. He said, "I don't like Cokes at all!"

I said, "That's great! That really looks good on this commercial."

There was a gentleman outside of Murfreesboro named Bill Perry who had a farm pond. It was probably about an acre or so, and I had heard he had a lot of big fish in it. So I called him and asked if I could go out there and maybe do a show, fishing from the bank He said, "Sure, come on!" We went out there and caught some of the biggest bass you could imagine. With every cast, you'd have get a fish at least five, six, or seven pounds! I asked him how he got all those big fish in there. "Well every time anybody catches a big fish, they come by, and I buy it from them. Then I put it in this lake." I did the show, and I had seven bass on the stringer, and none of them would go less than six to seven pounds. When the show was over, I released them all in front of the camera. Boy, that was great!

Perry had this pond fixed up really nice. He had a well, and when you pushed a button well water would spurt up out in the middle of the pond. It helped cool the water and make fishing even better.

Jimmy Holt from Nashville, Tennessee, had the *Tennessee Outdoorsman* fishing television show. It ran on a Nashville station for many years, and I did many shows with Jimmy. We were fishing on Percy Priest Lake one day and decided we would move across the lake to another place. I had a guy up in front, running the trolling motor, so I hopped behind the steering wheel, and we headed across this part of the lake. Jimmy looked over at me and said, "I can't believe it!"

I asked, "What is it you can't believe?"

"I can't believe I'm sitting here in this boat, and a blind guy is driving us across the lake."

I turned to him and said, "It's my boat, and I'll drive if I get ready!"

I did a television show up on Center Hill with Jimmy and many celebrities from Middle Tennessee State, including the president, the head of the cafeteria, and several other dignitaries, including the baseball coach, Steve Peterson. We were fishing Center Hill that day with live minnows. The boat was pulled up on the bank, and I had a rod out the back of the boat. While I was standing on the gravel, talking with Steve, I asked, "Steve, is that line running off that reel?"

He looked around and said, "It sure is! This guy here has heard a bass run from twenty feet away!" I often wondered, *Did I really hear it, or did I just imagine that I heard it?* So I can't swear it is the truth, but I did catch the fish. A friend, Paul Cantrell, was standing close, and he also swears I must have heard it, because the line was definitely coming off the reel. We were going to have dinner on the houseboat that night so we carried everybody in but a couple of us, and we went back out fishing.

Jimmy Holt was a big believer in Stren Line. I guess the company gave him quite a bit of Stren Line. I, myself, was a Berkley person. So before we carried Jimmy's reel back in, I took it and stripped off all the Stren Line and filled it up with Berkley. Of course I didn't tell him about it. I wonder if he ever figured it out.

I did many *Tennessee Outdoorsman* shows with Jimmy, and we had a great time. We also had a lot of mysterious things happen to Jimmy. Sandy White and I were doing a television show with Jimmy, and Sandy hooked a fish. When he reeled it in, there were two lures in its mouth, and one of them was Jimmy's. He hadn't even realized he'd had a bite, but Jimmy got the "twice-caught" fish on film.

During this time, I had the television show, radio show, and newspaper articles. I was becoming known as someone who could catch a few fish even though I was blind. I started getting calls: "Would you like to come to this particular fishing club?" It may have been in Nashville, Shelbyville, or Lebanon or anywhere else, and I'd go as a guest speaker. I spoke to the Percy Priest Bass Club in Nashville, and at the end of the year, they voted on who was the best speaker; they had twelve speakers that year. I was voted as their best speaker, and I was guest at their Christmas dinner. I thought that was a great honor.

We did television shows for three or four years, but it got to be tough. Then channel thirty-nine was sold and moved to Nashville, which made it even tougher. We had to go to Nashville to put our shows on the stations down there, and it was quite expensive compared to what we had been paying. So we had to give it up.

CHAPTER 17

CHARACTERS

One of the great things about fishing is the people you fish with along the way. I've been fortunate in that I have had fishing partners from all walks of life and they have enriched my life tremendously.

Valmar Womack

I've had many great fishing partners, and Valmar Womack was one of the best! I was working up at Friedman's at the time, and this elderly gentleman, who was from Woodbury, Tennessee, but living in Murfreesboro, and I got to go fishing together. He was a nice old gentleman, who was retired from Broadway Express. He taught me a lot about Percy Priest Lake and a lot of places to fish, though sometimes it's hard for me to remember some of the places he and I fished. We fished out of Elm Hill, which is on Percy Priest Lake, and did quite well. As a matter of fact, for several years we won more money than anybody out of Elm Hill dock.

They had a Tuesday night tournament, and every time we'd go down there you'd hear somebody say something, "Guys, don't count your money until the old guy and the blind man come in, because if you do, you're going to come up a little short." That was a compliment, and I really appreciated it.

Mr. Womack was another guy I fished with who didn't seem to mind or act like I was blind. If he needed something, he'd ask for it, and I'd do it. There were even times at night when I'd tie his hook and sinker on, because it was a lot easier for me to do it.

Mr. Womack and I fished on a Monday night, and he and his son fished on a Thursday night. We were coming back into the dock one Monday night and he said, "Mike, I know where there is some fish, and I need to check them for Thursday night."

I said, "Okay! That would be good. Let's go check them." Well he drove around in the middle of the lake; he drove here, and he drove yonder and then he finally pulled up and stopped. I asked, "Is this where they are?"

"It sure is!"

Guess what? I cast out and caught one. I said, "Well they're still here. We might as well go."

He said, "Okay."

"I know exactly where we are!"

"How do you know where we are?"

"Not too far away is a little boat dock over there, and when it bangs against the bank from the water, I know exactly where we are."

"See! See! See! I was going to tell you, knowing all along you were not going to tell me!"

Mr. Womack knew the lower end of Percy Priest Lake like you know your living room, and he and I were a successful team. He knew the places to fish, and I was fortunate enough to help him catch quite a few fish He and I fished for several years, but he had a little bit of a health problem, and we had to quit. He sure was a great guy!

Algie Woodard

I also had a fishing partner named Algie Woodard. Algie was a very exceptional person. He was the kind of guy you'd say, "Well what time are we leaving?" and he'd say, "We should have left yesterday." He was always ready to go fishing and was a great fishing partner. Woodard was not big in stature, but he had a lot of charisma, and everybody liked to talk to him.

He and I fished for many years on Percy Priest, and he really knew the lake. I guess the reason he knew it so well was because he spent most of his time on it. Woodard and I would crappie fish all winter and bass fish all summer. Woodard was like all the rest of the fishermen I fished with. He didn't pay any attention to whether I was blind or not—he just wanted me to catch fish.

Woodard and I fished a lot of night tournaments—I'm talking many years. When he'd check to see if he needed to retie his line and would pull on it, and he'd say, "Oh it's strong! It won't break!" And the next thing you knew, he set the hook on a fish and bam it'd break. So it got so that every time he lay down his rod, I'd check it. If it needed retying, I'd tie it, so he wouldn't have to worry about it. I guess one reason is he didn't want to tie it on is you'd flip on the light and then you couldn't see until your eyes adjusted. Then he'd have to hunt for his glasses.

He had more tales than we could write a book about. We came in after fishing all day on Lake West Point in Georgia, and the guy helping us do a television show down there, his wife, and sister cooked supper for us. We were sitting out on the deck, and Woodard got to telling this tale. Woodard grew up down there in Sheffield, Alabama, down there on the river, and he hunted and fished all his life. Woodard was catching quite a few fish, and this gentleman wanted to go fishing with him, so Woodard finally agreed to go fishing with him.

At night in those days, you didn't use a light; you were afraid the light would scare off the fish. Woodard said he was going down this bank to fish, being really careful. And all of a sudden, he looked and saw a light flashing all over the bank. It was up in the trees, down in the water. He turned around and asked this guy, "What in the world are you doing with a light?"

The guy said, "I'm looking for boogers!"

"Boogers?"

"Yeah!"

"Cut that light! You're going to scare the fish!"

Well Woodard turned back around and then the guy said, "There he is! There he is!" Woodard turned around, and guess what? Something fell off of the bank and hit the water with a big splash. Woodard said he was excited and turned around to get the flashlight. But the guy in the back of the boat had abandoned ship. Old Woodard turned around and saw this big old head turned around by the edge of this boat. He had no idea what it was, so he grabbed his boat paddle and went to whip it. Woodard said he had about a toothpick of a boat paddle left when he finally found the flashlight, and it was a cow. The guy had hit the cow in the eyes with the light, and she couldn't see what she was doing and fell off the bluff into the water. Woodard said that was his last trip with the booger hunter.

Algie and I were doing a crappie show; we did several of them together. When we got through, we still had time to stay out on the lake, so I told the cameraman, "Neal, you can lay the camera down and start fishing, too." So he laid the camera on the floor and fished and fished. Guess what? He didn't turn off the camera, and all the things we were saying during this time—we were ragging him about different things—were on this tape. Some of it wouldn't necessarily be something you would want your wife or girl friend to know about you. It so happened this woman he was going to marry helped him edit the tape, and you can imagine what was on there. It was hilarious to us, but not to him.

Woodard and I were fishing on Percy Priest one night, and he was throwing a little fly. Well he caught this big catfish. It was a great big thing, probably nine or ten pounds. He got him close, and I reached to get this cat. Of course I couldn't tell if it was a blue cat or a yellow cat. But when it bit me on the finger, I knew it was a blue cat; yellow ones won't hurt you. I pitched the fish back in. I said, "Woodard, you caught him, you get him out!" So he reached down to thumb the fish, and it bit his thumb and drew blood.

Woodard had a son, T. C. Woodard, and he and I fished several tournaments together and did quite well. T. C. was also a great fisherman. I have always been amazed that here I am, old, blind, and there's nothing else wrong with me, I hope, and there is always someone who wants to go fishing. I suppose there's not many blind people bass fishermen are always excited to go fishing with and compete with them in a tournament.

Considering some of the tales I put in the paper about these guys around here, I'm surprised I'm still running around. Woodard and his fishing partner at that time, Neal Thornburg, were fishing a tournament on Percy Priest Lake. It was cold, and the wind was a howling! They got out of the van, walked around the back, and they decided right quick and Woodard said, "You know, we don't need to be down there fishing." So what I put in the paper about Algie Woodard and Neal Thornburg going fishing was about them going around the back of the truck and the wind blew up their dresses, so they both ran home.

On another trip, Woodard was fishing, turned around, and fell out of the boat. So what did I put in my column? I put in there that Woodard stepped on his skirt tail and fell into the lake.

I was doing a *Tennessee Outdoorsman* television show with Jimmy Holt one day. Woodard and I decided we'd take him crappie fishing. Well we were fishing up at the lake, and Woodard and I decided before we got there that if he caught one crappie that'd be good, and if he caught two, we would move. Guess what? We stopped at this place where we knew there were some crappies, and Jimmy caught one. I told Woodard, "That's one!" We kept fishing, and he caught another one. "That's two, Woodard!"

Woodard said, "Well, I guess we've got to move!" So up we left. We went to another place, and we caught crappie. Jimmy caught one. I told Woodard, "That's one!" Then Jimmy caught another one. I said, "Okay Woodard." He laid the trolling motor down, and off we went again.

We did this three or four times. Finally Jimmy asked, "All right, you guys, what in the world are y'all trying to prove?"

I told him, "We're trying to prove that you can only catch two crappie in one place and then we're going to move." Guess what? He had lots of rebuttal for us about what we were doing to him. This was all on his television show, too, by the way.

You could start a medical book on the things that were wrong with Woodard, but you'd never know it by the way he fished. He would fish constantly and was always ready to go. Woodard had two open heart surgeries. He and I were fishing one day, and he said, "I'm going to have to quit. I just can't go. I'm really in bad shape."

I said, "Woodard, you can have another open heart surgery."

"No, they told me I couldn't. Two was all I could have."

"When we get back, you contact your doctor and then let me know that they can't do it again."

Woodard contacted his doctor, and guess what? They were able to do it again, and Woodard got probably another eight or ten years of life that he wouldn't have otherwise had. Whatever the ailment or problem, you could ask Woodard, "Well, how are you doing, Woodard?" He'd say, "If I was any better, there'd be two of me." You would know all along that he was feeling really bad.

There has been a fishing tournament established out of Fate Sanders Marina each year in Woody's honor. It's called The Woody's Tournament, and they made it an all-night tournament. People used to say, "Woody can fish all night." Well that was wrong. Woodard would fish for about half of the night and then he'd sleep about half. Then he'd come in primed to go, and everybody thought he'd been up all night. Woodard passed away several years ago, but he's always in our memory, because he was always full of jokes and was a great fisherman.

Erwin Cole

When I started fishing the BASS tournaments, my fishing partner was Erwin Cole. We both fished the tournaments and didn't fish together except in practice. Erwin was a Murfreesboro angler, and he and I traveled many hundreds of miles going to fishing tournaments around the area. One of the things I learned about fishing from Erwin was to be self-sufficient. Erwin never treated me as though I was blind. He treated me like I was anyone else, and you had to do your part of the work. I guess that's what helped me become a whole lot better fisherman than I was before we started fishing together. We had the opportunity to go places and fish with different lures on different lakes, and there was always something new.

There were always questions wherever I went. "How can you fish?" I always told them, "I guess the reason I can fish is because I'm good!" I didn't tell them how many hours I spent trying to be a halfway decent fisherman. They were always interested in how I tied on my lures. Well most of the time, I had to show them. I would lay the eye of the hook on my tongue, take the line, and stick it through the eye. Then I'd tie it. It's very easy once you learn how. One person who learned quickly and continues to do so even today was Erwin. This is how he ties on his lures. When we'd have night tournaments on some of the area lakes. I would usually wind up tying the other guy's hook for him, because when you'd turn the light on to see to tie it, you were temporarily blinded. We'd both be blind. That doesn't work, because somebody needs to be fishing.

I was in Florida fishing a BASS tournament with Erwin, and I was holding the boat. Well being dumb, I had one foot on the little dock and one foot on the boat. Some guys came up, talking about what they'd done. You know, being a nosey fisherman, I wanted to see. I wondered, *Well maybe they'd been doing something I didn't do, and I might learn something.* I was concentrating and listening to them when Erwin backed the trailer in and bumped the boat. Guess what? One foot wanted to stay on the dock, and one foot wanted to stay with the boat, but they both parted company. Down in the water I went! It was every bit eight inches deep and I thought sure as the world I was going to drown before I could get out. These guys I was listening to said, "Now Mike, if you're going in the lake, you need to have your life preserver on!" I did not have one on at the time.

I guess one of the saddest days of fishing was many years ago in a BASS tournament, when we were fishing on Lake Eufaula. Erwin and I were practicing down near the dam, which was quite a ways from where everybody else was. We came out of this little creek—I believe the name of the creek was Black Creek—and the wind must have been running from north to south and was howling. As we went around a point, there were swells that were eight feet high; those are some tremendous waves. By the way, I wasn't standing up then. We'd hit a wave, and water would come over the nose of the boat and fill the boat up. Well I propped my feet up on the rod locker, and we kept going. We finally managed to get back to the dock. Along the way, we saw boats pulled up on the bank and boats sunk, but we managed to make it in. I guess this was one of the sadder times in fishing.

A man was out there fishing, and he ran out of gas. He went back to change his tanks. He had his life preserver apparently wrapped around his arm, and he got knocked off the boat by a wave. He drowned. In the meantime, his wife was waiting for him back at the state park on Lake Eufaula. A very sad time for fishing. If you are going fishing, be sure you wear a life preserver correctly!

I was fishing a tournament up in East Tennessee. It was the American Bass Fisherman tournament, and it was called the Big Bad Fortieth. Whoever wound up in fortieth place got a new boat. Erwin and I were fishing up above Cherokee Dock. As we were standing up in the boat, going around this bank and fishing, I heard this bird whistle. So I whistled back at the bird. I like to hear birds whistle. Well the bird whistled, and I whistled. We did that two or three times, and Erwin said, "Here it comes!" Erwin turned and looked up, and this big eagle was coming down. I mean he was coming! He pulled out right over me, and I could hear the wind in his wings as he went flying by. I bailed off the back of the boat and got down in the bottom of the boat. The eagle went way up high—way up—and then he came again. He did that two or three times, and Erwin jumped behind the steering wheel, and away we went. But that eagle was still mad at us. Erwin said, "I don't know what you said to that eagle, but it sure got his mind messed up!"

Jerry McKinnis

In 1977, many things happened that made me feel quite good. Jerry McKinnis, who was the co-host for a television show called *The Fishing Hole*, called me and asked if I would do a fishing show with him on Center Hill Lake. *The Fishing Hole* was one of the more prominent shows in our county, and I told him I would be delighted to do so. We went to Center Hill and stayed a week. It rained every day, and as far as filming a television show, this was not a very good time. We came back to Murfreesboro, and Jerry said he would give me a call in a week or so.

I received a call from Jerry about two weeks before Christmas. He was sending his plane to pick me up at the Murfreesboro airport. We flew to Little Rock, Arkansas. From Little Rock, we went to Lake

Ouachita. Can you imagine flying in a twin-engine plane not knowing exactly where you are going, having never been there before, and having never flown in a twin-engine plane?

We landed in Little Rock and proceeded to Lake Ouachita, where we had a cabin already set up for us. We went out and practiced for several days and then went out and did the show. I understand the show was quite good—it was also very unusual. At that particular time, I was not too familiar on how you went about doing a television show, but I learned a lot in those two weeks I spent with Jerry McKinnis.

For one thing, you wear the same clothes each day. It may take two or three days to do the show, but it would appear like you've done it all in one day. It was cold, the temperature was tough, and the wind was blowing, so we wore coats. That was the reason nobody knew we had fished more than one day to do that television show. Jerry was a great host. I had known him for several years, because I was in the sporting goods business, and he attended a lot of the shows.

Don Phillips

Then along came Don Phillips. Don was a fireman, working for the Murfreesboro Fire Department. He and I also fished out of Elm Hill and Fate Sanders, and we did quite well for many years. He also taught me a lot about Percy Priest. He grew up in that area and knew a lot about the lake. We fished alike, we caught a lot of fish, and everybody started worrying about whether we were going to beat them in each tournament. He and I had some exciting times.

Don was a very unusual person. He was one of those guys who chewed tobacco and spit everywhere we went. We were fishing this tournament one night, and Don hooked this fish, but it got off. Don spit, "Sputt, sputt, sputt," all around and then he got up and put on a new worm, and he threw out again. Well guess what? He lost another fish. He was really agitated then.

He got down, put on another worm, and added some Magic Formula that was, "Definitely going to catch a fish!" he said. Well he got another strike! The slick stuff he put on his worm was also transferred to his rod, and as he set the hook, the rod went into the lake. Don did his chore of spitting all over the place. Then he turned around and stepped down into the bottom of the boat. And guess what? He stepped in the middle of his tackle box, and his tackle went everywhere.

Well Don weighed about 250 pounds, and here I am, about 180. I knew if I laughed out loud, he'd probably throw me into the lake. So I turned my back on him. But it was hilarious. You have never seen anybody that was so excited. His lures were lying everywhere, and he was really working that tobacco over. But as you would have it, we moved to another little spot and caught enough fish to place second in the tournament, which was pretty good.

Tom Mann

I've been very fortunate. I've fished with some of the best fishermen in the world, including Tom Mann, who became a friend. Tom was one of the first promoters of fishing on Lake Eufaula, and he developed the Mann's Jelly Worm. Many times I would go to his house and get new lures he was making. I still have some he made and I've kept. Nobody else has got any like them.

Tom and I fished on Lake Eufaula and caught a tremendous amount of fish. Of course we were using a Mann's Jelly Worm, and it happened to be blue and eight inches long. We pulled up on this hump—there was another gentleman with us—and Tom was saying, "They're here!"

I asked, "How do you know?"

He said, "I can smell the shad."

I replied, "All I can smell is something that smells like sardines."

Well we started fishing, and I hung a fish. Guess what? He's still going, I guess because he broke my line. I did that three times before I managed to land one in the boat. But I did manage to catch more than my share of fish that day. I caught five bass that weighed over six pounds each. That's a pretty good day! We were just fun fishing and not in a tournament.

He had this private lake on his farm in Eufaula, Alabama. He had about a thousand-acre farm and a big lake. So I went over there and hooked my boat to his truck. My friend Sandy White and I fished his lake. We caught quite a few fish in that lake. I caught one bream that was so big Tom put him in his aquarium for everybody to see. He said that bream weighed a little over a pound and a half. That's a pretty healthy bream.

Tom became a good friend of mine, and I went down and talked with him many times over the years. He passed away a few years ago. He never said anything about me being blind, either, and I fished with and against him on several occasions. I also became friends with Don Mann, who was Tom's brother. It wasn't a year or so later that a tragedy struck there also. Don killed himself, which was a shock to everyone.

CHAPTER 18

FISHING

Being I am a fisherman and someone who really loves to fish, when I learned I was going blind, I started thinking, *How can I fish when I'm going to be blind? I don't know what to do.* I thought and thought, and then I thought, *You know when you're fishing, you're throwing under trees, around bushes, or whatever the case may be.* So I got out in the backyard and started practicing.

I would set a minnow bucket under a tree, and I would shut my eyes and cast at it. Well if I missed the minnow bucket and hit the ground, I knew I had missed. I did this hour after hour for many days. My garage door made a little noise when you hit it, so I would back up and throw at the crack at the bottom of the door. I'd go back maybe twenty feet and cast. Then I'd go back thirty feet and then forty feet, and that's how I learned to cast. It was a long, slow, and tedious process.

I would cast whenever I had an opportunity. In front of Mike's Sport Shop there was a little hall. I would set up something and cast at it. It might be a minnow bucket or just anything to cast at that might improve my accuracy. I became quite proficient. I could cast a certain distance; I didn't have to do anything but just say, "That's thirty feet." The time between when it left and when it got there was what I went by.

Everything I did in fishing I had to learn, because there was nobody to teach me what to do. When you put a hook on, there's a certain way that I do it. When you run the line up through the guides of your rod, there is the way I have to do it. For everything I do, I have worked out a method, so I can be productive and not cause any problems for anyone else.

During this period, I fished with many fishermen. I learned a lot from them, and they said they learned something from me. I don't know what it was, but it probably wasn't catching fish. Blind people have one bad problem. That's their equilibrium. They can't stand up; they weave or they bob almost constantly, because they don't really know what looking straight forward is. As I mentioned before, I am one of the most fortunate people in the world, because my equilibrium is excellent. Only once or twice in all my fishing escapades have I been known to get dumped into the water.

A lot of times when I'm fishing with these guys, they do everything they can to make me throw into a bush or in the wrong place, but it doesn't take long for me to figure out exactly what I need to do. I fished with this guy one time, and he did everything he could think of to make me throw into the bushes or hang in a tree. It didn't happen. I didn't throw into one single bush or get hung in one single tree. He could not understand it. He came back into town and was talking to a group of fisherman. He said, "Mike Lorance is not blind! I did everything I could to make him throw in a bush or hang up, but he never did once." This fisherman didn't know how much time and effort I put into learning to miss those trees and bushes. I had many ways of finding out where these guys were throwing so I wouldn't be taken advantage of for just the heck of it.

People started contacting me, wanting to know if I'd be interested in fishing with some of their equipment or something else that would help their business. I was always glad to do that, because the merchandise was free. One of the first sponsors I had in any of these tournament trips was Berkley. They provided me with rods and line—all I wanted. As a matter of fact, they even paid my entry fees for some of the BASS tournaments. I was also placed on the staff of Hummingbird. I knew the president. I'd met him a time or two, and they sent me new depth finders. Anytime a new one came out, I would receive it.

I had heard all my life how easy it is to fish. You don't have to put forth a lot of effort. It's a lazy man's sport. Well let me tell you, If you get out there and stand up in the boat all day and fight the waves and fish hard, when nighttime comes, don't anybody have to rock you to sleep. You're ready to go to bed.

We were caught out in a big storm one night. There were waves six or eight feet high, and water was coming over the boat, but I was never scared. When we came in, some people asked, "Well, how did you handle that? Were you scared?"

I said, "No, I wasn't scared. I had a life preserver on, and I could swim. I could hear the water hit the banks, so I knew if I got tossed out of the boat, I could swim to the bank and wave until somebody picked me up. If they didn't come, I'd sit out there and holler and scream. Sooner or later, somebody would come and find me."

I learned at an early age that water is dangerous. You don't have to be afraid of it, but you definitely have to have a respect for it and know what it can do to you. When you go to the lake, take precautions. Be cautious, and don't do things that you are not equipped to do.

Anytime somebody would ask, "Would you like to go fishing?" Most of the time I would agree. I didn't have too many ask me to go hunting, though. That seemed to be something they weren't too excited about doing.

After all my practicing, fishing came easy to me, and I was invited to go to many functions. They had a big fishing expo at Middle Tennessee State University, and I was invited to be one of the participants in it, which is an honor. The students who attended received credit, like they had gone to a class at the university itself. I thought being invited to this function was extremely nice, and I was really pleased about it.

I helped start one of the first bass clubs in Rutherford County. It was the Murfreesboro Anglers. A lot of the local anglers were in this, and we had a lot of fun. I learned a lot about fishing that I probably would not have been able to learn otherwise.

We had some great speakers come in. Since I was one who selected the speakers, I guess they'd better be good. Some of those I managed to get to speak to the fishing club were Tom Mann, who developed the

Mann's Jelly Worm; Jerry McKinnis from *The Fishing Hole;* Stan Sloan, who would become the owner and producer of the Zorro Minnow Baits; and Glenn Wells, who was one of the top BASS fishermen for quite a long while.

They discussed a lot of things about fishing I didn't know. I never said much and I took in everything. I acted like I didn't know what they were talking about, but I continued to listen until I learned everything I could possibly learn. I had begun to fish a lot of local tournaments, especially night tournaments, and was becoming quite proficient at it. As a matter of fact, I was winning quite a bit of money!

Billy Westmoreland was a friend and one of the top smallmouth fishermen in the world. He was renowned for the number of huge smallmouth he caught on Dale Hollow Lake. He and so many other people helped me in many different ways over the years. They were friends, and when I needed someone to go fishing with or for a television show, they were always willing. Most of these guys have passed on, but they have left their mark on the fishing world. I am proud to have known them.

The Lions Club in Murfreesboro has a fishing tournament every year. One of the few organizations that I really helped was the Lions Club, because they do everything they can to help blind people. In these fishing tournaments, I try to find sponsor monies for them. Each year I wind up collecting more money than anybody else, which to me is great, and I am sure they appreciate it. I also fish in the tournament, and the best I ever finished was second. That's not good, but it sure beats third or whatever else is down the line. Each year I've always been able to come away with more money than I invested in entry fees, which is a pretty good thing.

In my time as a fisherman, I have owned approximately twenty-six new boats and motors. Everybody wonders why. Well I was able to purchase them at a cheaper price because I was so successful as a fisherman, even though I was blind. That's one of the benefits of having your own radio and TV shows. I have sponsors that have done many things for me. As a matter of fact, I have several even today from where I can buy rods, reels, line, boat, motors—you name it—at a reduced price. I think that is one of the best things my notoriety has done for me. It keeps my fishing tackle up to date, and I don't have to worry about it.

I entered tournaments early, and I had many great fishing partners. When you're fishing a tournament, you need a good partner. Someone who is blind definitely needs a good partner. One of my first partners was James Taylor. He was later known as "Booty" Taylor. James was like me. We were both very ignorant in the ways of tournament fishing, but as time went on, we learned more about it and became a little more successful.

When we had these pot tournaments years ago, it was sort of like a shotgun blast; everybody lined up, and away we went. Well everybody knew I was blind, and as we were going out to the blastoff, a friend of mine, Erwin Cole, and I switched seats, so I was driving the boat like everybody else. One guy turns to this other fellow and asks, "Pete, was that Mike driving that boat?" James said, "Booty! It sure was!"

He was known for saying booty in almost every conversation and that's how he got his nickname Booty. When we got to the blastoff, I turned and went to the right side, and guess what? Everybody was lined up on the far side of the river. There was nobody close to us. So when they hollered, "Go!" I jumped up and switched seats, and we were so far ahead of everybody else it wasn't even funny. Everybody was afraid to take a chance I might run over them.

I used to always tell these guys, "Now guys, my fishing partner is handicapped, and he needs at least two to three pounds extra just to be able to compete with everybody out there." But to this day, nobody has ever given us an ounce, much less two or three pounds! When I fished with some of these guys, they'd do everything they could think of to hide, so I wouldn't know where we were fishing if they were competing against me in some other tournament. But I would usually base where they were from the sounds I would hear, for example, which direction I would hear the boats going. If I heard a boat going down the lake, I'd ask, "Is he headed toward the dock?" or "Where's he headed?"

It is hard to remember all the people I fished with, and I'm afraid I might forget someone and then I'd be walking down the street and they'd threaten me. I have fished many tournament trails, including Professional Bass Fishermen (PBF), Sports Outfitters, American Bass Fishermen, BASS, and the Edd Rogers—he had a Chevrolet dealership in Sparta, Tennessee. In none of those tournaments have I had any problems fishing with anyone. Most people don't even consider me blind, which is a great compliment! I fished the PBF circuit for many years and fished with several fishermen. There was Erwin Cole, and we did quite well and made the classic several times. I fished with Sandy White for several years, and we also made the classic several times. I fished with Dick Pruitt, from Murfreesboro, and we also made the classic several times.

When you stop to think about it, there's a blind guy, and he's fishing with everybody on a lot of lakes in a lot of states, yet he has someone to fish with him. Either I was considered a very good fisherman or a very lucky person, one or the other.

Everybody I fished with in the night tournaments said, "Oh, you've got an advantage. You can feel better than we can."

But they have black lights and everything else to help them see in the dark. I answered, "No, I don't really think I have an advantage. You can see your line, and you can see when the fish hits and which direction he's going. I have to guess a lot of times, because I'm not sure where he's going." When you cast out and they move the boat, the line moves. But you have to keep up with your line, and all these things create a problem unless you do it an awful lot. Most of these fishermen are very considerate at night. If there's a tree in the way, they'll tell me about it, because unless there's a wave hitting the bank or something, I don't know there's a tree there, and I have been known to throw in trees.

One thing I learned over the years is that I do not need any help when I get into the boat. I stand up and fish most of the time, I tie on my own lures; I usually have my lures arranged where I can find them when we head for the lake. I don't ask for any help from any of these fishermen. Most of the guys just don't realize how hard it is to get to the position I'm in. It took a lot of hours of fishing and a lot of hours of hard work, and I guess maybe a little determination.

The main thing needed to catch a fish if you're blind is concentration. You have to concentrate. You may be talking to your partner, but you're usually not as noisy and talkative as others. You have to be conscious of what's going on. If something happens to your line, you feel something that's different. All these things come into play when you are fishing with an artificial worm or a jig at night. A spinner bait or something like that is no problem, because of its constant movement, and you can feel the fish when it hits. A lot of people let their eyes dictate as to what they are going to do. If they happen to look away and they get a bite, they don't really realize it until it's too late. Most of the guys I fish with don't give me any advantage. As a matter of fact, they really hate for me to beat them, and I have on occasion beat most of the guys I fished with.

Billy Westmoreland, from up on Dale Hollow Lake in Celina, and I fished several times together. That was an experience, but he never once said, "Well it's great to have a blind guy fishing with me." He always said, "Boy, it's great to have you out here!"

My fishing experiences have been great and varied. I have fished with so many different people it's hard to imagine—some of them great fishermen, some of them not so good—but I have enjoyed every one of them. I was fishing Center Hill one night with the vice president of Emerson Electric Corporation. His name was Gary Barton. He and I were going down this bank, fishing. I did know a little bit about Center Hill, because I had fished it before I had gone blind. As we were fishing down this rocky bank, I heard a milk jug hitting against the bank. I said, "Gary, see how close you can come to that jug that's bouncing off the bank over there." Gary reared back and threw the cast. It sounded as though he must have missed it by thirty or forty feet. I said, "I believe I can do better than that, Gary."

He said, "Okay! Hop to it!" Well I figured about where it ought to be, cast, and hit it. Gary said, "I bet you can't do that again!"

I drew back, cast, and hit that sucker again. I said, "I tell you one thing, there will not be a third try!" By the way, this was night fishing, too, not in the daytime.

Usually when I'm fishing with someone and they catch a fish, I net the fish. If we're lucky enough to win, I don't care who catches them; we split the pot! I was fishing with Dick Harris, a local fisherman from Woodbury, Tennessee. He hooked this fish, got it up to the boat, and it jumped. Being a lucky netter I am, I just flung the net out there and caught the fish in the air. Dick said, "Boy, that's a good fish! It'll go between four and five pounds."

"Yes," I said, "but you didn't catch it! I did!"

I've been fishing with Mike Walker from Murfreesboro for many years. Mike has a problem: he can't hear. But I can't see. Other fishermen ask me, "How in the world do y'all communicate?" or, "What happens?" I explain, "Well if I get mad at Mike, I talk about him, and he can't hear me. If he gets mad at me, he makes faces at me, and I can't see him. That way, we get along fine. He's also an excellent fisherman."

Roland "Hoppy" Hopkins, owner of Fate Sanders Boat Dock, was out cleaning some fish on the dock one day. Well he was trying to do something, and he was filleting a fish. Guess what? The fish jumped into the lake with his knife. Hoppy looked around, and he didn't think anybody saw him. But he was mad as a hornet, because the fish got his knife. That's a strange turn of events. He thought he was going to eat the fish, but the fish ran off with his knife.

Anytime anything funny happens or somebody does something they don't want everybody to know about, I put it in my column, as long as it doesn't hurt their feelings or their reputation. I have people call me all the time, telling me things that so and so did. I might not know about it until they call, but I usually have a place to put it. I put that in the paper about Hoppy losing his knife to the fish, and he sure got a lot of flak out of that.

Fishing has opened a lot of doors that I would have not even known existed. People remember that I am blind, because they've either competed against me or have read or seen something about me. It is very exciting to know people remember you. Erwin Cole and I went into a small outdoor shop in Clearwater, Florida When we entered, a man said, "Hello!" And after a few minutes, he said, "Oh you're Mike Lorance! I've heard of you!"

Erwin asked me later, "How do these people know you?"

I said, "Erwin, I don't know. I guess word gets around, so they have to tie everything down. They're afraid I'm going to pick it up and run off with it."

Erwin asked, "Do you know everybody?"

"Only the ones who are important, and that's everybody I know."

It's hard to imagine the fishing innovations we have now and how things were when we first started. When we first started fishing, we were using old crank reels, old fishing poles; you cannot believe the equipment we wound up using. I think the first fishing reel I purchased cost fifty cents or a dollar and half, which was like a week's pay at that time. Now you have casting reels that run over five hundred dollars. If you drop one of those in the lake, you better go in after it.

I think I am one, or maybe the only one, who can put a hook and sinker on the line going down the lake at sixty-five miles an hour at night. It doesn't make a difference whether it's daylight or dark, I can do it either way. One of the toughest things for most people to do is put on the Carolina rig. You have a bead, sinker, swivel, and a tag line. Putting on the sinker is hard enough for most people, and putting on the little bead is terribly hard even for those who can see. They can hardly hit that little hole, and they didn't even have to put on the swivel. Well I can also do this speeding down the lake. I am very fortunate to have the dexterity to do this.

Well I'm not a spring chicken anymore, but I still fish night tournaments two to three times a week. And I still have some awfully good fishing partners, and we do quite well. My partners and I were fortunate enough to make the classic on the PBF tournament trail many times. I guess you'd say my partner was the reason we made the tournaments, because he drove us there and ran the boat. All I did was catch a few fish occasionally.

Chapter 19

First Tournament

In those days, the top fishing tournament in the country was the Bass Anglers Sportsman Society (BASS). Ray Scott was the founder and president at the time. While I was working for John Friedman, there was an outdoor show in Nashville, and I stopped at a booth, and in there was Ray Scott. I asked him, "Ray, I sure would like to fish some of those tournaments that you have."

"But," he said, "I really rather that you didn't, because since you're blind, you might cause some problems, and I might lose some interest."

I said, "Well okay."

I left feeling a little downhearted. The more I thought about it, and being the sorry individual I am, I thought, *Nah, I'm going to fish some of them just to show him that I can.* I sent him money for my application, but instead of putting Mike Lorance on it, I put Ervin M. Lorance; they didn't know Ervin, but they did know Mike. Guess what? I was approved to fish the tournament on Lake Tohopekaliga (Toho) in Florida.

I went with Erwin Cole, from Murfreesboro. We rode down and practiced. On the day we had to register. Erwin said, "You just follow me, and I'll show you where to go." Just as we got to where we had to go, they split us up. He went to the right, and I went to the left. I thought, *Aw, man! What am I going to do now?* I eased down the line, following the guy in front of me until he stopped. A woman said, "Sign right here!"

I asked, "Sign where?"

"Right here." I reached down, followed her hand, and signed.

I went by the tournament director, Harold Sharp, and shook hands with him. He gave me a little box, which I had paid three hundred dollars for, and away I went. He never knew I was blind. The night of the drawing—they say it's a drawing, but I think it's a parity—Erwin and I were talking, and Harold Sharp said, "Erwin! Erwin, come here! I've got to talk to you!" I thought, *Uh oh! This is trouble!* So Erwin went over there, and I could hear them. Sharp asked Erwin, "The girl that filled out his form said he acted like he had a little problem seeing. Are his eyes bad?"

Erwin said, "Yep."

"Can he see?"

"Nope!"

"He's blind?"

"Yes."

"What am I going to do?"

"I guess let him fish!"

"I don't know how to do that! No telling what might happen."

"Well he told me if he doesn't fish, then nobody's going to, because he's going to get an attorney and get an injunction." I hadn't said that, but that was all right. because that took care of the deal. Sharp agreed I would fish the first day, and if I didn't cause my partner any problems, then it would be all right.

In the first tournament draw, I drew one of the top fishermen from Louisiana, Bo Dowden. He had done really well in these tournaments. They called my name and told me who I was paired with. I went up to meet him. I shook hands with him, and a few words were passed. I was fishing as a professional. In other words, we all paid the same fee. In the competition, each fisherman spent half the time at the front of the boat. We stood there and talked a minute. and I said, "Now Bo, there's something I need to tell you."

He asked, "What's that?"

I said, "I'm blind." There was a long silence. He didn't know what to say. I said, "Don't worry! Everything will be all right!"

Bo answered, "Okay."

The next morning we went fishing. We ran from Lake Toho all the way down to Lake Kissimmee. We went through a lock and about fifty miles away, we went into this lake. We went from Toho to Hatchet Hall, Cypress Lake, and down into Lake Kissimmee. We were fishing behind this island. I caught a couple of fish, and Bo caught some. When we got ready to leave, he said something about where we were. I said, "I know where we are fishing."

"You do! How do you know?"

"I was here before. I fished this lake before."

"You're not going to tell anybody, are you?"

"Well no, I'm not going to tell anybody." The next day was so rough we couldn't go back, so it didn't make any difference whether I told.

I was preparing to fish another tournament. I think this one was in Eufaula or some place in Alabama—I have forgotten—and I sent off for my application. Erwin Cole called me and said, "Mike, has anybody read this application to you?"

"Well no, they haven't."

"Well you listen to this. It says up at the top, 'Are you known by any other name other than the one above?'"

"Uh oh!"

Erwin read a little further, and it said, "Do you have any physical defects? If so, explain."

"Oh they got me!"

He read further, and it said, "'We reserve the right to refund anyone's money that we think would be a handicap to his partner.'"

"Uh oh, looks like I've been had."

They had changed the wording on the application, so they could take care of me. Bright and early the next day, I made a call to Montgomery, Alabama, to the BASS headquarters. A woman answered the phone and I said, "I'd like to speak to Harold Sharp."

"Well Mr. Sharp is not here. Can I help you?"

"Well I don't know. I'm Mike Lorance."

"Oh we've been expecting your call."

"You have?"

"Yes we have."

"What have you been expecting?"

"Harold told me that any BASS tournament that you wanted to fish you were more than welcome to do so."

So that sort of wound up that ball of yarn, and I fished several after that. I did quite well in them, as a matter of fact. I placed in the top one hundred out of three hundred anglers several times. I fished one tournament where someone asked that I be his partner for one day, and I was. I thought that was pretty neat, too. He said he'd seen me in the tournaments and had always wanted to fish with me. We fished on the Kentucky Lake. So I guess maybe I helped blind people when I did all that.

CHAPTER 20

BASS ANGLERS SPORTSMAN SOCIETY

F ishing became my hobby, and that's how I became known as the "blind fisherman." Some people may think that sounds bad, but it didn't make any difference to me as long as they were talking about me catching fish. I fished tournaments all over middle Tennessee. If there was a tournament close by and I had someone to go with me, away we'd go! Many times I thought how great it was that though I am blind, people wanted me to go with them as a tournament fisherman—fishing for money of all things!

This was about the time I started fishing the BASS tournaments, and there were some exciting experiences in this particular stretch of my life. I was quite successful for a blind person, and many of the tournaments included the top fishermen in the United States. There were often 250 to 300 entrants, and I placed in the top 100.

I have had the honor of fishing with and against some of the best fishermen in the country. I drew Jimmy Houston, who is a big television personality now, in the tournaments. I also drew Stanley Mitchell, who won the Bassmasters Classic. I fished with Tom Mann, Billy Westmoreland, Celina, Tennessee; Hughbie Green, Chimney Rock, Tennessee; Leo Breckenridge, Knoxville, Tennessee; and Bo Dowden. Another person I fished with was Jerry Brown. I fished with too many to name them all, but they were almost all really good guys, and they were all great fishermen.

I remember one time I drew Jimmy Houston in a tournament on the Saint Johns River. We rode in the boat for twenty-three minutes. He stopped the boat, shut it off, and we started to fish. I said, "Jimmy, I've been here before!"

"You have? How do you know?"

I said, "I've fished this place before."

He said, "Where is it?" I told him, and he said, "I can't believe that!" What he didn't know was Erwin Cole and I had fished this in practice, and I knew exactly where it was.

As the day went along, Jimmy hooked a fish, and in those days, we were allowed to use a net. Well the fish jumped, and I jumped for the net. Then I turned around and said, "Ah, you don't need a net."

Jimmy asked, "What do you mean?"

"I heard him jump. He's not twelve inches long." That was the limit in those days. Well Jimmy got it in the boat, and guess what? The fish wasn't twelve inches long. A little bit later, Jimmy hooked another. I grabbed the net and got it down to the fish. "That's a keeper!"

Jimmy asked, "How do you know?"

I said, "I heard him jump!" I netted the fish, and sure enough, it was.

Jimmy was standing up front, fishing, and said, "I wonder what the water temperature is."

I said, "It's sixty-eight degrees."

"How do you know?"

"I put my finger in there!" Well he went directly back to the console of the boat, looked at his temperature gauge and then went back to fishing at the front. I asked, "What was the temperature, Jimmy?"

He never said a word. A little bit later, he said, "Sixty-eight degrees." If anyone's ever heard him on his television show, he's got a cackle, and that's how he cackled that day.

Jerry Lokey and I were fishing one night on Center Hill Lake. Jerry has a problem seeing at night. As a matter of fact, he has a terrible time seeing at night. His wife was afraid for us to go because of his problem. We went anyway. We picked out an area to fish and Jerry said, "We can't get lost from here!" So we go over and were fishing from the bank. We were doing quite well but if we didn't pay attention, he couldn't see the bank with the black lights. So I would listen to the crickets and tell him where to go. We followed this bank and fished until daylight. When daylight came, we were in good shape, so we went in. We came in second in the tournament.

When we went back around to the cabin, my wife and his wife were both sort of antsy. They wondered if we were going to make it, or if we were going to get run over, or if we would run over someone. But we came in with a little money.

Another person I drew in these tournaments was Ray O'Breckenridge. One thing I found out after I started fishing with him on this particular day was that his wife was blind. So during that day of fishing, I had a very good time.

There was a fisherman from Memphis, Tennessee, who everybody in the country has heard of. It was Bill Downs. I got to know Bill quite well. I was standing up by the board one night, trying to find out who my partner for the next day was. He slipped up, put his arm around me, and asked, "Who is this?"

Teasing, I said, "Roland Martin!"

Bill said, "I tell you what I'm going to do. If you call me Roland Martin again, I'm going to throw you in the lake!" There were alligators in that lake, and I definitely didn't want to go in with them.

I drew a gentleman in a BASS tournament on Lake Eufaula. I don't remember his name, but he had fished three days of practice and two days of tournament and not caught the first keeping bass. Well I'd managed to catch a few, so I wasn't really feeling all that bad. We left that morning, and he said, "I know a spot where I'm sure I can catch a bass. Somebody told me about a brush pile."

I said, "Okay, we'll go there then."

So we went to where he thought this brush pile was located. He circled and he circled and he circled and finally said, "It's got to be out here somewhere." He stopped and put the trolling motor on. Guess what? The first cast I made I hit right in the brush pile and caught a keeping bass. He said, "I am ready to quit! I'm ready to go home. I haven't caught a fish, and it's now the sixth day, and you just sat there and caught one I just knew I was going to catch! I'm going home!"

I said, "No, let's don't go home! Let's go fish!" I told him I knew a place where we'd found some fish during practice. "Let's go there." We went there, and I caught another keeper. Then I caught another one. Then he caught three fish in a row that were about six pound apiece. He got a check and all I got was a lot of, "You did goods!" I didn't get any money!

I drew this one fisherman who had just won the Bassmasters Classic a short time before. We were fishing down this ledge, and the guy must have thought I was dumb as well as blind. He had the nose of the boat pointing into the ledge where I couldn't reach it, because he had the boat the first half of the day. Guess what? I got into my tackle box and got me a larger sinker for my artificial worm. And when we weighed in, I had more than he did. That like to have killed him. Somebody asked me how I enjoyed fishing with him that day. I said, "Well it wasn't bad. He tried to keep me from catching the fish, but that's what he's supposed to do."

While I was fishing these tournaments, I got to know a lot of very nice people, including Forrest Dale Wood, who was building Ranger boats. I had dinner with Forrest and his wife, Nina, one night, and he told me, "If you ever need a boat, you call me, and I'll see that you get one." Fortunately, I never did need one that I couldn't afford to buy.

I drew this professional fisherman one time named Hughbie Green. He's passed away, but he had this little article out about his fish-pointing duck. Hughbie claimed he had this duck that would only point out big fish so he could catch them. He also put in there that he didn't take him to Florida or any place down there, because he was afraid the alligators would get him. I drew Hughbie in a tournament, and we were working through some grass. I turned to Hughbie and I said, "Hughbie, I do believe we have a leak in the boat."

"How do you know?"

"You got cans floating around back here in the back of the boat." We had gone through the grass and had pulled the plug out of his boat, and water was coming in through the drain plug. The water wasn't cold, and I definitely didn't want to go swimming with the alligators down there on a Florida lake. So I ran to the front of the boat, and he went to the back and put the plug back in. We continued fishing.

When I was fishing BASS, I fished with some of the greatest fishermen in the world, including Stanley Mitchell, who I drew in one tournament. He had just won the Bassmasters Classic. Guess what? I beat him!

These guys just couldn't stand it when I beat them, but it was exciting for me, because it meant I had done my best and that people were not thinking of me as a blind person but as a fisherman. There is one thing I always tried my best to do: fish as hard and as long as I possibly could. A lot of times you'll see fishermen sitting down, "Well, I'm tired." I never did do that. I just kept fishing, even though I might be tired. In those days, tournaments were for six days. You had three days of practice and three days of tournament—that's six days of long, hard fishing. Though BASS tournaments were long and hard, they served their purpose for me. They let people know being blind didn't mean you could not do a lot of other things.

We were fishing a BASS tournament on Kentucky Lake many years ago when Ray Scott, who was running BASS, came to me at the end of the second day and he said, "Mike, be ready to leave when you come in tonight."

I said, "Hah, I'm not going anywhere! I've got to fish tomorrow."

"You be ready to go, and we'll pick you up. We've got places to go." Being inquisitive, I thought , *Well I'd better go. I don't know what Ray's got in his mind.*

We went to the Paducah, Kentucky, airport and got on, of all things, a Learjet. I've ridden in some speedy little vehicles and some pretty good airplanes but never anything like a Learjet. I'm sure you've heard, "Man, he took off like a jet!" Well that's the way this jet took off. We left Paducah, and in forty-five minutes, we crossed part of Kentucky, all of Tennessee, part of Alabama, and we landed at the Eufaula, Alabama, airport. I don't know how far that is, but brother, it was a quick trip.

The reason we were in Eufaula—Tom Mann, Bo Dowden, a couple other tournament fishermen and myself—was that we were all guests at the Alabama State Park at Eufaula, Alabama. They were having a big dinner there, and we were all invited. That was a great occasion to all, especially to me since I was blind; and all the rest of these guys could see and they were all good fishermen. I was just a tag-a-long. I don't know who got me in on that deal, but it was a great experience. Can you imagine—poor, old, blind fisherman many, many miles from home, with strange people, and not knowing where anything is? It was an experience I still remember. Of course, there were plenty of radio interviews and a lot of people from the paper who were putting all this down for the local news and probably other areas. These are experiences sighted people have very little opportunity to participate in, much less someone who is blind.

After the dinner we headed back to the airport. Once we got to the airport, they had the doors to the hangar open and the pilot said, "Nobody open the door until we get out of the hangar, because if you do, the noise will burst your eardrums."

We taxied out of the hangar and got ready to go. I asked the pilot, "How much room does it take for us to take off?" He said some ridiculously low number, and I asked, "How long is this runway?" He told me, and I said, "Well you take it all!" That critter took off like a rocket, and it wasn't long until we were back in Paducah. After we landed, I went back to the campgrounds and prepared for the next day's fishing. I don't think I was very good that day. I was a little bit pooped!

It seemed that just about everywhere I went; newspapers or television stations would come by and want to interview me, since I was the only blind BASS tournament fisherman. The questions were usually about the same. How do you fish? How do you tie on your lures? How do you find your lures? How do you know how far you are going to cast? How do you cast around trees? When they asked how I fished, I'd say, "I learned to fish through practice. I practiced a lot—made a lot of mistakes—but as I went along, I corrected a lot of those mistakes." When they asked how I got my lures prepared I would say, "My wife helped me pick out the colors, and I put them in my tackle box a certain way so I'd know where everything was. If I picked up one, I knew it was good or I wouldn't have put it in there to start with, so I had confidence that whatever I picked up would catch fish."

I've been asked what type of fishing equipment I use. I try to use the best I can get. I use spinning rods and casting rods. I am also able to use the fly rod and flipping stick, so there's not many things I don't use. I'm very fortunate in that I've had a lot of companies sponsor me, provide me with equipment, and pay my entry fees in the BASS tournaments.

I was, and still am, the only blind person to fish a BASS tournament, which is a great honor. People have asked me if I get any help. No! If they could, they probably would make you miss every fish that ever bites. They give competitors no help whatsoever. As a matter of fact, as you are about to step out of the boat, they might want to give you a little nudge. These guys are fishing for big bucks, and they don't want any competition at all if they can help it. I will have to say there were some really nice guys in those tournaments that I fished in who really went out of their way to help me. But I didn't need any help. I had everything worked out before I got there.

These experiences are hard to forget. Not many people have the opportunity to do what I was able to do with the Bassmasters, and they were exciting experiences. Though I didn't win tournaments, I did scare the fire out of some of those guys. Most of these fishermen really hated it when I came in with more fish than they had. "There is a blind guy, and he caught more fish than I have." They think it's really bad, but maybe it was because I was fishing a little bit harder than they were.

CHAPTER 21

MEXICO

A couple of us decided we wanted to go fishing in Mexico at Lake Guerrero. At that time it was the hottest lake in the world, or so we thought. Dave Lawson, Billy Andrews, and I decided we would go, so there we went—all the way across Texas in a motor home and all the way down into Mexico. When you cross into Mexico, you had better have Mexican insurance, because ours isn't good over there.

We fished on Lake Guerrero and caught a ton of fish. They called us the blind man, the preacher, and the devil. We were quite a group. One day we went out on Lake Guerrero with a guide named Paco. He was sitting and running the boat. He had on this big helmet. I asked, "Paco, why have you got that helmet on?"

He said, "You'll know." Well we were out there fishing, and all of a sudden, I heard something go *bam!* Billy Andrews had hit that helmet with a great big lure. We figured out very quickly why Paco was wearing the helmet.

We decided to go into town and have dinner one night in Victoria, Mexico, and I had my arm on Billy Andrews's shoulder. The street was very narrow, and there was a light pole there. I dodged the light pole, but unbeknown to me, there was a piece of steel sticking out at the bottom. Guess what? It hit me right on the knee. I did a lot of hollering and a lot of rubbing it. I sat down on the steps and was really doing some rubbing when the Mexican police pulled up. They looked at me and one said to the other one, "Drunken gringo! Drunken gringo!" So they drove on by.

When I finally recovered enough to go hobbling down the street, we went to the hotel where we were going to have dinner that night. The gentleman who ran the camp where we were staying told us it was the place to go. Well we went up the steps, went inside, and then went down some steps. It was explained to me what it looked like. From their descriptions, it looked like the old hotels in the westerns, where there is a main floor with balconies all around the sides.

We had seats in the middle of all the tables—there weren't any other customers—and we ordered our dinner. I couldn't decide what I wanted so I considered the waiter's suggestions, and then I thought, *Well I'll get me a piece of steak.* So I ordered a piece of steak. When it came, we looked at it. On my plate were beans and everything else you can think of—and things we couldn't identify—and right in the middle of my plate was a piece of steak about the size of a dollar bill. I said to myself, *I know everything around this steak is hot. I don't believe that steak is that hot.* So I proceeded to cut off a piece. Guess what? It was so hot it made my lips turn inside out. I started hollering for the waiter, "Beano! Beano! Beano! Mucha quick!"

The waiter brought me some wine, and Billy Andrews, who is a preacher, asked, "How in the world did you get that wine?"

While we were having dinner, a man was playing the piano. He was the worst piano player in the world. I don't believe anybody could have been as bad as he was. He was playing "Tie a Yellow Ribbon 'Round the Old Oak Tree," and he was messing it up. He couldn't play "Jingle Bells" and make it sound like "Jingle Bells." When he got through and everything was quiet, and I thought, *Well, you know that fellow did his best,* so I started clapping for him. He started playing again, just as sorry as he was before, and Dave Lawson said, "Mike, if you clap for him again when he gets through, we're going to leave you in this hotel!"

We all wanted a shower when we returned to camp. But there was no shower except in the motor home, and we did not want to use up our water. This camp was very, very primitive. They had two outside privies, and everything the guy who ran the camp owned was under a parachute. That's also where they lived—under this parachute. We decided we were going to take a bath, and when the locals all left, we decided we were going to take a bath in the lake.

The reason we wound up at this camp was when we stopped to get our license from this fellow, who was a game warden, he had asked if we had a place to stay. We said, "Not yet."

He said, "Follow me!" Well in Mexico, if you do something wrong, they can confiscate everything you have. We thought he might try to confiscate the motor home, so we decided we had better follow him. And that's how we wound up at this primitive campsite.

While we were there, we decided to go to town and see if we could buy some boots. We went into a bootery, but he couldn't understand English, and we couldn't understand Spanish, so we had a hard time negotiating. I came out with a pair of leather boots for eighteen dollars. Don't ask me how I wound up paying eighteen dollars, but we did negotiate. Dave Lawson came out with a pair, too. I think he paid twenty dollars for his.

We met a lot of people while we were at the camp. Most were Mexicans; we didn't see a lot of other tourists. The majority of them could not believe I was blind. They'd wave their hands in front of me and do a variety of things to see if I was really blind.

Fishing the area lakes in Mexico is a unique experience. People use cans for reels instead of regular reels. They'd have about forty- or fifty-pound test line wound on the reel. They would take spinner bait and throw it by hand. The poor fish didn't have a prayer. When someone hooked a fish, it was coming to the house. When we went out on the lake, there would have two or three in the boat. One would be rowing, and one of them would be trolling. He'd hold the can out there, with the bait behind it. It's something to see.

When we'd start out on the main part of the lake, we had to follow ropes to get out to the center part of the lake. We didn't know where we were going, so Paco went with us once. When we went again, we'd take some rags and tie on the posts at the corners of the rope trail, so we'd know which corner to turn on the way back in. We were in the middle of all these bushes and trees. When they made this lake, they just filled it in, and everything that was already there was underwater.

We had our best day of fishing in a corral. The water had covered a horse corral or cow corral or whatever it was, but the fish there were about three or four pounds, and they would hit just about everything you threw, so we had some exciting days.

As we were leaving Mexico and headed toward Tennessee, a border guard asked, "What do you declare?"

We all declared, "We're broke!" And that's how we got through the border. They looked through everything and found nothing. They agreed we were all broke and were allowed through.

It's a long way from Tennessee to Lake Guerrero in Mexico, and it's even further on the way back. But we decided we'd go through New Orleans. I had never been there. We got down on Bourbon Street, and I was this blind guy, walking through there and looking around, though I couldn't see anything. But we did all right. The only thing I didn't like was they said this lady was going in and out of a window down there. I didn't know it was a dummy, but that was what it turned out to be. Everybody else was looking at it, and that was one downfall.

Of all the places we went, including Mexico, I never got sick. We went into this place beside Al Hirt's club down and had shrimp. Guess what? I got sick. That night we were in the motel, and Dave Lawson said, "Mike, let's see what they got around here; we might see something and maybe have us a little mixed drink."

I said, "Okay!"

Billy Andrews slept in his motor home so Dave looked out the window of our motel room checking to see if Billy had gone to bed. He said, "Well he's asleep, so we'll go on." We went out and all of a sudden Dave said, "Lookie yonder! Billy is peeping out the window, watching us!" We went to a club right around the corner, and it was pretty nice. We came back, and that was the last we ever heard of that, but I thought that was right funny. Billy was peeping out the window of the motor home, watching as we left.

CHAPTER 22

SAINT THOMAS

Ruby and I took a trip to Saint Thomas. As a matter of fact, we went over more than once. I decided I wanted to go out fishing. We went out and made arrangements to go fishing the next day on a boat. We got on the boat and went out of Red Hook Harbor on Saint Thomas Island. The sea was a little rough but not bad. There were four of us on the boat. I'm standing over by the railing, and this guy asked, "Would you like to troll on the way out?" I said no.

So another guy got up there, and he was trolling. The first mate came by and said, "You'll be the only one fishing after a while."

I asked, "How do you know?"

"I just do!"

"Where are we going?"

"We're going out to the drop-off."

"Drop-off! What kind of drop-off?"

"It's about seven hundred feet on the top and about fourteen hundred feet on the side."

"That's the place I want to go!"

Well, the first mate was right. It wasn't long until the woman who was with this other guy was hung over the side, and he was, too. The one who was sitting up in the chair trolling was over on the other side. Guess what? I was the only one fishing.

We hadn't been gone too long, with me sitting up in the chair, before I caught this big tuna fish. I finally got that dude in, and they said it weighed about seventy-three pounds. So here we go! Later in the day, I caught an eight-foot sailfish. I was still sitting up there, fishing, and since nobody wanted the chair, I kept fishing.

About one or two o'clock, I hung a blue marlin. I have had a lot of fish on the end of my line, but not like this dude. The fish hit, and the first mate said, "Wait just a minute. Now set the hook!" The reel was about the size of a washtub and had one-hundred-pound test line on it. I was buckled in the seat, and the rod was buckled to me. Still, this fish was peeling the line off, and the only thing I could think was, *Where is my knife! If this fish jerks this seat out, I don't want to go with it!* After I hooked that dude, he jumped. I didn't see him jump, but brother, I could hear him jump! And then he came toward the boat, just as hard as he could go. So, we started going the other way and that big old—washtub reel, it must have been about one ton—crank, crank, crank, crank; that's about the way it was. Then the fish turned and went the other way. The rod went down, and it was about like holding onto an automobile after it jumped. I said, "Man!"

The first mate was standing beside me and he said, "Looks like you're going to be here about two hours."

I said, "Let me tell you something! You look at me real close, because this dude won't be in this chair two hours from now. I or this fish—one has got to go!" Well guess what? It was the fish that left first. He jumped and spit the hook, and I was never so happy of anything in my life.

As we were on the way in, they had three flags that you flew when you were successful. They had a tuna fish flag, a sailfish flag, and a marlin flag. The captain had two of them flying. I asked, "What's wrong with the marlin flag?"

He said, "That's when you bring them in."

I said, "Let's run that marlin flag at half mast, because we got him part of the way in!" When we got back in, Ruby and Dot came down and got pictures of the fish. That was my first marlin to hook and you can betcha' it will be my last one!

I have been very fortunate over the years. I have been a lot of places. I've been from Saint Thomas to Canada to the Rockies to Florida to North Carolina, and all the areas in between.

Chapter 23

Heart Attack

I fished several Professional Bass Fisherman (PBF) tournaments with Dick Harris, and there is one I really remember. It was in May of 1991. We were about twelve miles from Goose Pond, on Lake Guntersville, Alabama. I started feeling rather bad, so I told Dick, "Let's go back toward the dock. I don't feel really well." We were fishing about a mile from the dock, and I said, "Dick, let's go over in this little causeway that goes over to the park. I'm hot!" When we got there, I got on the back deck and reached down to wash my face. "Dick, go to the dock—I'm having a heart attack!"

To the dock we went. I managed to get from the back of the deck to the front deck, but that was as far as I could go. The emergency squad arrived and got me out of the boat. I couldn't get out on my own, and the only thing I remember was a voice coming over the radio that said, "ETA twelve minutes." I thought, *Twelve minutes—that's not too long.* And that's the last thing I remember.

When I finally came to, I looked over to the door I heard somebody. It was Dick coming in the door. "Dick, what in the world are you doing here? You need to be back out there fishing! We need to win a little money. We're both broke. Hurry up! Good-bye!"

When I came to again, this time in the emergency room, a guy and a woman were standing over me. "What's going on?"

He said, "You're having an infraction."

"What in the world is that?"

"A heart attack. I have something that will help you, if you are willing."

"What is that?"

"A TPA shot." In medical terms, this is known as an Alteplase TPA injection.

"What will it do?"

"Well if you have a weak blood vessel in your brain, you will die."

"If I don't take it, what will happen?"

"You'll probably die."

"Well let's try the shot."

He gave me two shots, and the next thing I remember I was headed to Nashville, Tennessee, in a helicopter. I came to and thought, *You know, the doctors have done all they can do, and I've done all I can do. Now it's up to the Lord, and if he decides he doesn't want me, maybe I'll be around tomorrow.*

When I came to again, I was in Saint Thomas Hospital in Nashville, and a woman was trying to put a needle in my arm. She was punching two or three little holes and I said, "Hey ma'am, I'm not going anywhere." But she did—she couldn't do it anymore and she had to leave because that liked to have scared her to death. They had to get somebody else to give me a shot. I had a heart attack, and it had taken out the back of my heart.

I found out later that when I was in the emergency room in Scottsboro, Alabama, the nurse who took care of me was named Ruby. That was my wife's name.

They put me in the intensive care unit, and this little girl came by that night. She said, "My name is Trish." Well, my daughter's name is Trish.

I said, "Look here!" Ruby was looking over me in the emergency room, and here's Trish in the intensive care unit. So I pulled through in good shape. As a matter of fact, this happened on a Saturday. On Wednesday I walked the treadmill, and I went home on Thursday. I was ready to go fishing the next Tuesday night. When I got home and was able to get out and around, I sent the lady in Scottsboro, Alabama, named Ruby some flowers. I thought she deserved them for just having to put up with me. This happened in 1991, and I am still fishing with Dick Harris, so that must be a good omen.

CHAPTER 24

LIVING LIFE BLIND

As I look back over the last several years, I find that my life has really changed. In 2005 my mother passed away. in 2006 my wife passed away, and in 2007 I lost a guide dog. So guess what? My role really changed. You talk about adjustments, there was quite a few adjustments for me during those three years. I became someone who took care of the house, the cooking, the washing, the cleaning—whatever was necessary I had to do. You do not realize just how much help your mate is until you do not have one.

When I started doing all these other things, I learned there was a lot I didn't know that I should have already known. Everything became a new challenge. I had to learn to cook things I had never cooked before, though I was able to do quite a bit before my wife passed away. There's one thing I can say, though. My light bill went down, because I didn't use any lights. I could do as much in the dark as I could in the light. People would say, "You must not have been home, because there weren't any lights on." I'd remind them I don't need any lights!

I've had other fishermen ask me at times, "Well, how do you keep your boat clean? What do you do to clean it?"

I say, "Well I clean it after dark. That way, people don't watch what I am doing."

My wife taught me many things. One of them was to be self-sufficient—do whatever you can do and do it as well as you can do it. When my wife passed away, that left a lot of responsibility to me, since I was the only one here—just my guide dog and me. I had to learn how to clean the house thoroughly. I didn't want a dirty house if anyone came in it. I knew a lot of this stuff, but it was never a "have-to" case before. I learned to clean bathrooms, commodes, sinks—you name it, and I learned to do it. You have to come up with ways to do things sighted people do easily. They're not easy for someone who is blind.

I can relate to what women have to go through. Brother it's tough! Cleaning seems like a never-ending chore. You clean house this week, and next week it's as bad, or worse, than it was to start with. There's something to do constantly, and you're never caught up—dishes to wash, floors to mop, and rugs to vacuum.

When I vacuum, I usually go over it once and sometimes twice to be sure I don't miss anything. When people come in, they say, "Oh your house is so clean." They don't know how many problems I had getting it that way. Have you ever tried to vacuum under a table, but you don't know where the table is? Well it's a challenge, but it can be done.

I had to learn to wash clothes. Every time you change clothes, you look down and say, "Uh, that thing is really getting full of clothes. I've got to wash clothes." My wife would always tell me, "Be sure you have clean clothes on and that they match before you leave home."

After she passed away, this fell on me, so I bought shirts and pants that matched, so regardless of what I picked up, they would go together. Then there was the matter of socks. How am I going to keep my socks separated? How am I going to know which is blue, brown, black, or whatever? In this case, you pin them together when you pull them off, and when they are washed, you fold them together.

I hate dirty dishes. I hate to pick up a fork or a spoon in a restaurant and find it is dirty. So when I wash mine, I am extremely careful. I do not want any dirty utensils to come out of my house. If I have someone over, I want them to find clean utensils, clean plates, and hopefully, good food.

Then it came time to eat. Well where's my cook? I don't have a cook, so I have to do the cooking myself. I know why my wife used to ask me, "What do you want for supper?" I didn't know then, and I don't know now, and I'm sure everybody goes through the same thing. It was really tough thinking about what to eat every night. I now know what problems women have.

I've learned to cook. It may not be the best in the world, but when you're the only cook, it's as good as you're going to get. A lot of times I have people come to the house—maybe several. In a case like that, I'll have a caterer sneak in, but I'll take credit for preparing all the good food.

When I clean windows, I have to clean them at least twice, because I don't know whether they're clean the first time. I look and don't see a thing on them.

I try to be sure the outside of my house and yard look good, and I've had people tell me I make the rest of the neighborhood look bad because I keep mine so neat. I don't do that myself most of the time—I have someone else do it.

My wife used to tell me she did the yard work and I did the inside work. Then she had an idea. "I can tie a rope to this tree, and you can go round, round, round and just work your way back in, until the rope stops. Then we can move you to another tree." You know, we didn't get around to that, but I would not have been surprised if she had not slipped up and tied a rope on me.

People ask me, "Who reads your mail for you?" I have a scanner, and when you scan a typewritten page through, it tells you what it says. If a piece of mail is handwritten, I get my daughter, Trish, to read it to me.

Since my wife passed away, I have made an extra effort to do things she would have wanted me to do and hope to make people realize blind people can have a fulfilling life. I've been told that I am the exception. I don't know what an exception is, but there are a lot of blind people who don't go out to restaurants or anywhere else. I do! I go everywhere!

Because I'm able to focus my eyes on whoever I'm talking to or whatever group I'm addressing, people sometimes don't realize I am blind.

Being blind does have drawbacks, but it also has some advantages. I was coming out of this restaurant not too long ago, and a woman came up and grabbed me. She was gave me a big hug and asked, "You don't know who this is, do you?"

I said, "No, but I'll find out in just a minute," even though her husband was right behind her and could have misconstrued my intentions as blind people see with their hands.

Guide dogs are an important part of my life. The main problem with being blind is your mobility. Everywhere you go you need help. In my case, whenever I get ready to go, I have a guide dog. This also opens a lot of doors for me. Whenever I have a special need for something, people remember me because of my guide dog. I got my first guide dog from Seeing Eye in 1968. I received the one I have now in 2007.

I have been to many places as a speaker. I don't know why they want me; there's always someone a lot better. But I tell them one thing: "I'm an expert on blindness and on guide dogs." I've had many years of experience.

When I was in my later teens, I received my senior life saving license from the Red Cross. In the late sixties, Ruby was taking swimming lessons at the Veterans Administration Sports complex, and I was talking to some of the instructors there. I said, "You know, I just wonder if I could requalify for my senior life saving license?" I had been blind for a few years.

The instructor said, "I am qualified to give you that particular test, and if you would like to take it, I'd be glad to give it to you."

"You know what? That would be outstanding, and I think I'll try it."

So I proceeded to attempt to receive my senior life saving license. I passed all the tests they had, but a couple remained. I had to swim the length of the pool and go down and pick up a block off the bottom in fifteen feet of water. It's a surface dive. I received no help, so when I thought I was close, I did a surface dive. There was the block on the bottom of the pool. I retrieved the block, carried it back to the end of the pool, and passed that test.

Then I had to dive into the water and save the instructor. He was fighting and struggling. Well you can imagine. I went up, heard him struggling, went down, turned around, came up behind his back, got him the way I was supposed to, and proceeded to swim the length of the pool. When I completed all these tests, I requalified for my senior life saving license! I thought that was a pretty good accomplishment. At the time, I didn't think it was a really big accomplishment, but looking back, I guess it was pretty good. I don't know of another blind person who has done this.

After my wife passed away in 2006, I realized all the things she had done for me. She pushed, plodded, encouraged, and showed me how to do things I didn't know how to do. After she passed away, I realized everything I do is because of the things she taught me many years ago, though I really didn't realize it at the time.

Over the years, I've been a guest speaker on many occasions and in many places. In most cases, I've been asked to come back. I was recently a guest speaker at a Lions Club. The woman who invited me was given an award for having the best speaker of the year. I think it is outstanding to speak to a group of people and they think you are the best speaker they've had all year. That sort of makes my ego balloon up a little bit.

During my years of professional fishing, UPI and Associated Press both did stories about me that I thought were great. But I guess one of the better things that happened to me was Paul Harvey spotlighted me on his radio show. A lot of this was strange to me. I was blind, but I had worked for many years to be able to do what I was doing, and it really didn't seem like a big deal, because I was able to fish.

I have been asked many times how I can tell how far I've cast my lure. Well with the experience I have gained over many years of casting, I can usually tell how far I am throwing by the time it took the lure to travel a certain distance. If fishing at night, you would cast and, by the sound of the lure hitting the water, you could tell how close to the bank you were.

When I go fishing with different individuals, they often do everything they can to make me throw in the bush. A lot of these fishermen will turn right, left, or whatever to get me out of ka-whack. That way they expect me to throw in the bush, and they can go back and say, "Aha! Mike threw in the bush!" Well I've been very fortunate over the years. When someone I'm fishing with casts, I usually know where they cast, and I can tell if they've turned the boat, so I know I don't need to throw in certain areas.

I own my own boat. I fish out of it a lot, and I fish out of other boats. People wonder if I can fish out of that boat. If it floats, I can fish out of it. I take care of my boat. I keep it washed. I keep it vacuumed. I keep all the electronics up to date. I keep everything about it good, and I'm sure a lot of people wonder about that also. You would think by now most people in my area would know what I can do, but I'm always under scrutiny. Do this—do that. Can you do this? Why do you do that? There are always questions, and hopefully, I will have the answers to most of them.

I don't care what you do, if you want to become proficient at it, a lot of work is required. You may be the best employee in the office, but most likely, you worked harder than the rest of your co-workers. You may be the best football player, but in most cases, you put in a little extra time to develop your skills. That is why I continue to work at what I do. I may get out and practice casting, or I may do other things to help my fishing ability.

I was told one time, "You never know who is watching you!" Whenever you are out doing something you shouldn't be doing somebody else may emulate what you are doing. So for that reason, I try to do my best at all times.

Remember the story of when I was the first person to bring a guide dog into a particular restaurant? You can bet that everybody in that restaurant was watching us. If we made a mistake, people would be quick to tell others, "I saw this blind guy do this," or "I saw this guide dog do that." There are a lot of people who sit back and talk about what this blind guy can't do. If I think I can accomplish something, I'll do it. I may have put forth extra effort, and might have to do it when somebody else is not around, but if I think I can do it I'll do my best to figure out a way to do it.

There's one thing about being blind. You can get lost anywhere. I don't care if it is in your own house or outside, you can get lost. Whenever I'm going outside to the back of the yard, I place the radio out on the back porch so I can hear it. That way I know there's where I need to go. There's home. I don't need to get lost out here. It helps me become even more self-sufficient.

Many people look at the things I have accomplished and think how great it must have been, but to me, these things were just everyday things, and I never thought anything about them. I am still involved in many of these activities. I am still invited to go to places and be a guest speaker. I still fish quite a bit. I would hunt, but it is sort of hard to hit a rabbit or squirrel when you can't see where it is going. All these things have made me enjoy my life, though there are problems and things that must be overcome. But it is still great to know people appreciate what I am able to do. When you're talking about fishing with a blind guy, I have had some of the best fishermen in the United States fish with me.

There's one thing everybody should remember: you are what you are. Don't try to be something you are not. Everything you do has choices. If you make a bad choice, you must suffer the consequences. If there's something you want to do and want to do it badly enough, you can be successful if you put forth the effort. Someone once asked me, "Do you know what a successful man is?"

I replied, "I'm not real sure."

He told me, "That's someone who, when he gets knocked down, gets right back up. If he gets knocked down again, he gets back up." That's the way we go through life. We're going to get a lot of knockdowns, but we have to get back up and keep trying.

Every phase of life has challenges. Looking back over my life, I see where I did make changes for many years. Now it's time to make even more. I'm still the outdoor columnist for the *Daily News Journal* in Murfreesboro, Tennessee, as I have been for the past thirty years. I still fish quite a bit, especially the night tournaments in the summer and crappie fishing in the winter. And in the summer, I sometimes go fishing just for the heck of it.

I have always loved to fish. As time progressed, I met an awful lot of fishermen who were a big help to me. They became lifelong friends. Whenever I needed something, I could always call them. When I was fishing some of the major bass tournaments, I got quite a few sponsors, and I am still associated with many of them. Whenever I need anything, there is always one of them who will be able to provide what I need.

I have written articles for *Bassmasters* magazine. Articles are easy to do. You are writing about something you really know, and it is easy to compile a decent article. The only problem is they often don't pay you what you'd really like to receive. I've been writing columns for many years, and they come easy. I have people who help me. I'll contact different people to get information to put in the column about the tournaments or anything pertaining to the outdoors. That comes easily, but doing this book has been terribly hard!

Another thing I've tried to do over these many years is to be friendly to children. You always run into children, and if you are nice to them, they will come back and talk to you as you grow older. They may say you were really nice to them. That really makes you feel good.

To progress through life there's one thing you've got to have: friends. I have made many friends along the way, and they have all helped me accomplish things in my life. Remember this: if you have a friend, take care of him or her, because there are not that many true friends out there.

If you were ever able to see, like I was, the things you remember have not changed. For instance, my wife looked the same to me forty years after we got married as she did when I last saw her, which was in the early sixties. My daughter looked the same, and most of the people I knew looked the same. In reality they had aged, but in my eyes, they had not.

I have been one of the most fortunate men in the world. I have been blessed in many ways. I had a wife who stood beside me for fifty-one years. Many times when you are alone, you start thinking about what could have been or what was not. But there is one thing that is always there and is a stabilizing factor. That is your belief in the Lord. Any time you have a problem, that's the place to take it. He says He will take care of you, and in all these years, He has really taken care of me.

I'm quite healthy and can fish all day and probably half of the night without any problem, while a lot of people my age are unable to fish at all and are unable to walk or get around. So I have been blessed in many ways with friends and with opportunities. Maybe I have helped make some of those, maybe I haven't. I look over my life and I think, *You know, I really wasn't as bad as I thought I was.*

CPSIA information can be obtained at www.ICGtesting.com
Printed in the USA
LVOW041658171012

303287LV00005B/6/P